Chasing THE *Wind*

by

William Boyd Chisum

M000211786

Chasing The Wind

©2006 William Boyd Chisum and Morgan James Publishing.
All rights reserved.

No part of this publication may be reproduced or transmitted in any
form or by any means, mechanical or electronic, including photocopying
and recording, or by any information storage and retrieval system,
without permission in writing from author or publisher (except by a
reviewer, who may quote brief passages and/or show brief video clips
in a review).

ISBN: 1-60037-004-7 (Hardcover)
ISBN: 1-60037-005-5 (Paperback)
ISBN: 1-60037-035-7 (Audio)

Published by:

Morgan James Publishing, LLC
1225 Franklin Ave Ste 325
Garden City, NY 11530-1693
Toll Free 800-485-4943
www.MorganJamesPublishing.com

General Editor:
Heather Campbell

Cover & Interior Design by:
3 Dog Design
www.3dogdesign.net
chris@3dogdesign.net

To David

May God continue to
use and Bless you for His
Glory !

"His Grace Is Sufficient"

William Boyd Thomas

Testimonials

Life is a journey. During my journey, I have had the honor of having William Boyd Chisum be a part. He is a truly special individual that mere words really can not describe. I had the fortune of working with Boyd and I wish I still did. He is one of the most genuine, hard working, caring and sincere individuals that I have encountered in my journey. Chasing the Wind only verifies the type of person I have known as a previous co-worker and friend. Being in the medical profession and even training for six months at Texas Scottish Rite Hospital, I am aware of the types of procedures and treatments Boyd encountered growing up. I was (and still am) amazed at his mental and physical strength to endure these treatments and still have a positive outlook.

His talents go far beyond being a musician, singer, songwriter, orthopedic physician assistant and (now) author. He has the ability to change people's lives for the best in many ways, but mainly by being Boyd. This may make no sense unless you really have spent time and gotten to know Boyd. I have and I am a better person. I have only been a small part of his journey, but I would not have missed it for the world.

Virgil B. Medlock, M.D.
Sports Medicine and General Orthopedic

When you are hurting, the cries of your heart seem to bounce off the heavens. When circumstances crush your hope, and only darkness of pain remain, what do you do?

Boyd Chisum's story helps us discover how to journey through the storms of life. His story leads us into the light and love of a Sovereign God who holds your pain and sorrow in His nail-scarred hands.

Though Boyd's life is challenged, God's plan and purpose is never displaced. What could Boyd have been if he had a "normal" life? Probably less than he is. It is out of our weakness that God puts His power on display.

The faith of Boyd in God was not the power to make things the way he wanted them to be; it was the courage to face things as they are for the glory and praise of God.

Dr. Charles L. Wilson
Senior Pastor, Sunnyvale First Baptist Church

In the Old Testament of our Holy Bible you'll find an individual characterized as "A man after God's Own Heart". David was his name and David's life as described in the scripture's was filled with the highest of highs and the lowest of lows.

Allow me to introduce you to William Boyd Chisum. Boyd is one of this generation's men that qualify for the same lofty description, after "God's Own Heart." You will be lifted toward the Heavenly Father as you turn page after page. God's movement in the heart of this unbelievably challenged child, young man, and adult will literally rivet you to the pages you are about to read.

Boyd is an accomplished writer, musician, singer, and most of all, loving father and husband. I am privileged to be his friend and to broadcast his music.

Charlie Campbell
KCBI-FM Dallas
Texas Gospel Music Hall of Fame.

Tex Ritter use to say, "The trouble with the world son, is everybody's trying to star in their own movie." Among other life stories, William Boyd Chisum shares with readers his exhilarating and disheartening experiences on the rollercoaster ride that is the music business in "Chasing the Wind," his personal and sometimes painful journey of faith. His rise in country music is full of chart records and rubbing elbows with the stars, but he reveals that success by music business standards differs dramatically from the satisfaction he finds in discovering the high and holy purpose God has designed for him. Overcoming his own personal desire for fame and glory, William Boyd Chisum has discovered true fulfillment in his walk with Christ. Readers will be challenged and inspired by this thought provoking chronicle of his life's lessons. "Chasing the Wind" is a powerful testimony of one man's life, the miracles, the wandering away and his glorious return to God.

Dave Moody
President, Lamon Records
Dove Award winning & Grammy nominated Artist, Singer
& Songwriter

Chasing The Wind

Dedication

This book is dedicated to my son Brock.
I love you with all my heart.
Daddy

Chasing The Wind

Preface

"Chasing the Wind" is a book about the grace of God applied to life.

William Boyd Chisum is an accomplished musician/singer, and an excellent songwriter, but he is more than that, he is a marvelous story teller.

In this book, Boyd tells the story of how God's grace rescued him from "Chasing the Wind" and delivered him into a life of service for Jesus Christ. To one degree or another we all have been given trials and/or tests -- For to you it has been granted on behalf of Christ, not only to believe in Him, but also to suffer for His sake (Phil. 1:29.)

Relatively few people have been called upon by the Lord to suffer a lifetime of the physical impairments that Boyd has endured throughout his life. But, in preparation for him to become a spokesman to deliver God's message, God says, "My grace is sufficient."

What Boyd communicates so well in this book is, "I'm a winner, and you can be a winner also by relying upon God's grace to guide you through your life." As he explains some the failures and successes of his life, your heart will break, but with the simple turn of a page those same tears of empathy will transform into tears of laughter. In the end, Boyd will bring you to a realization that the answers to life's quest are found in the application of divine grace to the circumstances of life.

I have spent most of my adult life teaching men and women how to communicate God's grace in a way that makes it applicable to life's experiences and circumstances. To become effective in that endeavor, one must define, describe, illustrate, demonstrate, and motivate the student concerning the subject of grace.

Boyd defines grace as that which God is now free to do for him based upon what Jesus Christ did through the cross on his behalf.

He describes how, by faith, at an early age, he received God's grace, gaining an assurance that, as a child of God, he knew his eternal destiny was determined and secure.

He then describes how he walked away from God's grace, choosing to go his own way, "Chasing the Wind," seeking, fame, fortune, and fans in the pursuit of stardom in Country Music

He then made a transition from using his enormous, God given, gifts and talents to become a celebrity artist in Country Music to excelling in the medical profession, which he accomplished with real class. But, as Boyd says, even that was "Chasing the Wind" and refusing to acknowledge God's grace in his life.

Boyd illustrates that his life of running from God's grace was an anomaly of extremes -- extreme debilitating pain, extreme physical handicap, extreme gifts and talents, extreme worldly success, and extreme spiritual failure – but, in the face of this anomaly, God's grace sustained him, in spite of himself, preparing him to become a winner.

As Boyd took up an intensive study of the Word of God, he began to learn how to demonstrate God's grace in his life. Boyd finally learned that 'chasing the wind' is to be replaced with the 'pursuit of grace'

Just as Solomon, the author of the book of Ecclesiastes, came to the understanding that self-centeredness is "Chasing the Wind," Boyd, along with Solomon, reports the solution is to become Christ-centered, by focusing on God's grace and the blessings that flow out of that dedication.

This book will motivate you to apply God's provision to the disasters and failures that exist within your human experiences and circumstances.

Boyd's message is, no matter how far you have strayed from God's plan for your life, no matter what kind of calamity you face in your life, no matter how sin has distracted your obedience to God's will for your life, God's grace is sufficient to forgive, restore, and sustain you in your desire to return to a worthy walk with Jesus Christ.

"Chasing the Wind" is a book about the abounding, amazing, marvelous grace of God and it has the potential to change your life.

In His Wonderful Grace,
Earl D. Radmacher

Earl Radmacher, is the General Editor of, "The NKJV Study Bible" from Thomas Nelson Publishers. He is a graduate of Dallas Theological Seminary (Th.M.,Th.D.) and served for more than Thirty years as President (later Chancellor and Distinguished Professor of Systematic Theology) of Western Seminary in Portland, Oregon. He now serves as president and/or board member of several Christian organizations and he also serves as President of Regal Grace, a ministry designed to help believers fully understand the grace of God and prepare for life in the coming kingdom.

Chasing The Wind

Foreword

Have you ever felt as though you were dealt a bad hand in life? Do you feel like all your life you have been living in a storm? Maybe you have been thinking of throwing in the towel and giving up.

We often take the most precious thing God has given us, which is life itself, for granted. We have been counting our lemons instead of our blessings. Then suddenly we run across something or someone who helps us get our life back into perspective.   That is exactly what happened to me when I read William Boyd Chisum's book, Chasing the Wind. Boyd shares with his readers about his continuous challenges and struggles in life. If anyone ever had the excuse to quit, it would be Boyd. After having over 60 surgeries on his hips and being hospitalized over 3,277 days of his life, which is almost 9 years, one would be tempted to ask the question, "Is life worth living?" Yet William Boyd Chisum has risen above all this and more and has experienced incredible victory due to his relationship with his Lord and Savior, Jesus Christ.

I have found in my own life's journey that the storms we face daily can beat down on us enough until we are blinded to any peace or victory that God wants to give us. But the apostle Paul said in Philippians 4:11, "Not that I speak in need, for I have learned in whatever state I am, to be content." One key to living above our storms in life is to learn to be content in the way we are. We wrestle with turmoil within ourselves because our human nature is to always want more. We compare ourselves to the next guy and believe we deserve what we think is "the good life."

However, when we learn to be content and trust in God's plan, we then rise above our daily storms. "For I know the plans that I have for you, says the Lord. They are plans for good and not for disaster, to give you a future and a hope." Jeremiah 29: 11. Our struggles take on a whole different perspective when we see them through God's promises. William Boyd Chisum has risen above the surgeries, hospitals and heartbreaks by trusting God's promises. In doing so, he has allowed God to use him to encourage others to do the same.

You are about to take a journey through a man's life that will challenge your own outlook on life. By the time you have finished reading Chasing the Wind, you will find yourself rising above your own storms. Enjoy your journey.

David Ring

Evangelist David Ring shares his story with over 100,000 people each year at churches, conventions, schools and corporate events. He has been featured on Focus On The Family, The Old Time Gospel Hour, and with John Hagee On Cornerstone. David Ring is in high demand through the Premier Speakers Bureau along with such notables as Astronaut Neil Armstrong, Colonel Oliver North, Comedian Jeff Foxworthy and two time Emmy award winner Deborah Norville.

Chasing The Wind

Acknowledgements

This book was written for Brock. Son, I just wanted you to know what it was like for me to grow up. My goal is to share with you my challenges, my failures, and my triumphs, so that no matter how difficult or sweet your life turns out to be, you'll understand that God's grace is sufficient.

Through the years many family members and friends have touched my life and help to shape who I am today. I am thankful for each and every one of you.

Mom and Dad, God gave you more challenges and heartbreak in raising me than most parents can even imagine having to face. Thanks for making the tough decisions when they mattered the most.

Bud Brown, you challenged me to dig deeper emotionally when I began writing this book. It was not easy to put into words all the emotions involved in living a life filled with physical challenges. Thank you for encouraging me to express what I felt at the time rather than just report what happened. Your suggestions enabled me to write a better book.

Heather Campbell and Kaylla Avant, thank you for the endless hours you spent in editing and making suggestions. All three of us know I would never have won a "Spelling Bee." This book would not have been possible without you.

Jack Moulton, it's been interesting. God has shown both of us that His grace is sufficient and that no situation is beyond His reach. Thanks for all the late night phone conversations and prayers.

And to Nena, thanks for always being the supportive "help mate" that you are. I can't count the times that your encouraging words drowned out my echoes of doubt. Here, there, or in the air. I will always love you.

Chasing The Wind

Contents

Chasing The Wind

Chapter  1

The Land of Oz

It started with a mother in early labor and ended in a way only God would understand. In those early hours of the night, a physician in the small Texas town of Lamesa, would make an irreparable medical mistake, unaware that God would reach out His healing hand of mercy to use it all for His glory. The mismatched blood transfusion, which I received that night, devastated my body in ways that my family was yet to understand. Escalating body temperature, little legs grotesquely swollen, and a tiny newborn baby packed in ice were just hints of things to come.

As time passed, the traumatic ordeal of my birth became a distant memory for my parents. All seemed to be normal until I reached eight months of age. My parents began to notice that, when I tried to stand up, I seemed to be in pain. When they would pick me up, the pain in my hips was intolerable. Red flags went up, and I was taken for x-rays to determine the cause of the symptoms. No one was prepared for the results that day.

The news was grim. The doctors surmised that the mismatched blood given to me the night I was born had caused such severe swelling in my legs and hips that the femurs were pushed out of alignment with the hip joints. As they grew, the femurs missed the hip sockets all together. This caused them to close over and the end of the femurs to be deformed. What a devastating mistake this careless small town doctor had made, but I know my God does not make mistakes. He is the Potter and I am the clay. The Bible says that all things were made by Him and for Him and, that includes you and me.

It was the great Ella Fitzgerald who coined the phrase "God don't make no junk," but the orthopedic surgeons looking at my condition might have disagreed. My parents were repeatedly told by one specialist after another that they had never seen anything quite like it before. It seemed impossible to find a starting point to fix a problem most doctors thought could not be fixed.

Finally, there was a doctor who told my parents that the only place in the country that could offer even a glimmer of hope was Texas Scottish Rite Hospital for Children in Dallas, Texas. He advised I would require a lifetime of surgeries and millions of dollars in hospital care. He said that, unless my dad was a multi-millionaire, Scottish Rite, a children's hospital that does not charge for treatment, was the only place for me to get the help I so desperately needed.

When I was nine months old, that beautiful building, with the white marble statue of a nurse holding a child, which stood at the front entrance, became my "on-again, off-again" home for the next sixteen years. The day my parents checked me in was a hard day, but I wasn't alone, God checked in with me.

Sitting in the auditorium, in multicolored plastic chairs, was a multitude of parents, nervously waiting for their names to be called. It was like waiting to see the Great Wizard, from the Wizard of OZ, to find out if you could get a heart or some courage, or even a little hope. But my parents were there to see if someone could help their child walk, and this wizard's name was Dr. Brandon Carrell, Chief of Staff at Scottish Rite.

After x-rays, blood work, and endless paperwork, my parents sat and waited, with distant sounds of cartoons playing on a TV that nobody, except the children, seemed to watch. Minutes turned to hours, as they stared at the doorway from where a man would eventually emerge, call my name and lead us to the one who held their hopes and my future in his large but gentle hands.

Charles, a man I would come to know well over the next sixteen years finally appeared in the doorway with a stack of x-rays in one hand and my chart in the other. He called my name and my parents and I were led back to the doctor's conference room. Dr. Carrell stood with a room full of surgeons as they studied the films, examined my legs and collectively decided that this was, indeed, where I needed to be.

As I recall the stories I heard about that day, in my minds eye, I can see him. Dr. Carrell was tall and thin with jet black hair combed straight back. His face was almost always in a fog of smoke from the pipe that he moved from side to side as he carefully pondered how to help you overcome your next hurdle.

Dr. Carrell had the ability to sense when a child was afraid. He would give them one of his special winks. His bushy eyebrows and piercing blue eyes seemed to say, 'it's going to be alright, I'll take care of you.' When those gifted hands held you and comforted you, it was easy to feel safe and secure. God used those hands to make life better for countless children, and I thank God for him still today.

It was settled. What could be done would be done. With orthopedics still in its infancy, and after the worldwide scare of polio, this hospital and its doctors were breaking new ground. They would do everything they could and hope that new technology would give them a hand down the road. They would try every new procedure known to man and even some that hadn't been invented yet. It was a staff of doctors shooting in the dark, but at least they had bullets in their gun.

Then my parents faced the most difficult and painful decision of their young lives. Could they leave me, their nine-month old baby boy, in the hands of strangers? After signing all the paper work, my mother and father placed me in Gods hands and walked out through the front doors, trying not to look back. Without this sacrifice, I am sure I would not be here today. Years later, my mother told me that she cried the whole ten hours of their drive home. It was a scene that would be repeated many times in the years to come.

William Boyd Chisum

Chasing The Wind

Chapter 2

The Imagination of a Child

My understanding of those events comes from stories my family told me. The never-changing day-to-day life at Scottish Rite Hospital that took place when I was too young to remember, would repeat itself day after day until I was old enough to recall events for myself.

Any familiarity in a world full of the unknown can be comforting to a frightened child. And I, along with the other children at the hospital, needed that in our lives. We liked the boredom of knowing what's next. It helped us get prepared.

My first few surgeries were corrective procedures, trying to repair my hip sockets. After these surgeries, I would be in a full body cast from under my arms all the way down to my toes. A wooden bar would be plastered between my knees to help secure the position of the hips. I would spend months in this cast. Body temperature inside a plaster body cast was sweltering. The sweat, mixed with the natural odors that come from a baby, made for many interesting smells and, I assure you, none of them were good.

I did learn, as I turned five or six years of age, that the body cast I was in made a wonderful garage for my Tonka trucks. The little matchbox trucks were fun to roll around on top of my cast and kept me occupied in my own make-believe world for hours at a time.

I figured out that I could place a car on my chest just under the rim of the cast and then suck in my belly and it would race into the cast toward my navel. When I was ready for it to stop, I would just push out my stomach, trapping the speeding vehicle against the roof of the cast.

This was fun until the day that little red truck took off like a demon, straight from the fires of you know where. It careened past the navel roadblock I had prepared and took a sudden turn to the left where it lodged itself near my left hip. Try as I might, I could not reach it with my hands. All I succeeded in doing was pulling out a lot of cotton padding that I would need when it came time to cut off the cast. The little red truck seemed to be permanently parked in its plaster garage. When I finally relayed the story of the runaway truck to the nurses, they were not at all happy with me.

I was too young to understand that an object like that in a cast could cause a pressure sore that could lead to infections. They tried cutting windows in the cast to locate the truck but to no avail. It was hidden and did not want to be found. The spica body cast was removed, a new one was put on, and my Tonka trucks mysteriously disappeared from my room all in the same day. I hope the nursing staff had fun playing with that runaway red truck.

William Boyd Chisum

Chasing The Wind

Chapter 3

Would They or Wouldn't They

I was able to go home periodically in those early years and when I did it was usually in a body cast. The cast was heavy and bulky so there was always a certain amount of planning that had to be done before my folks took me anywhere, even to church.

My parents sang in a quartet called the Kings Four, and I grew up singing and listening to gospel music. J. P. Skinner was our pastor at church and what a dynamo he was, and still is. My parents' favorite song must have been "Just As I Am" because they took me 'just as I was,' cast and all, to the church service and laid me on a cot or blanket at the back of the auditorium near the entrance. They would sing and J. P. would preach.

Brother J. P. would get all fired up in his sermon and ask the congregation if he could get an "Amen" and, from the back of the church, would come a little voice from inside a body cast saying "Amen." I became so good at it, I began to give them quite freely and, some would say, not always at the appropriate time.

J. P. Skinner still tells people today, that if it had not been for Boyd Chisum, 'I would never have gotten an "Amen" from anyone.' Later on in my life, at the age of ten, this same beloved servant of God led me to my redeemer Jesus Christ. Brother J.P. remains a dear friend today and is still preaching the truth of God's grace.

I wasn't able to see my parents as much as I needed or wanted in those early years. They had my older brother, James, at home to think of and there was no such thing as family sick leave back then. Visiting days at the hospital were only on weekends and were limited to only two hours. My parents would make a ten-hour drive one way and, before the wrinkles had time to shake out of their clothes, they had to turn around and drive another ten hours to get back home. They would get back to Lamesa just in time for my dad to go back to work after having someone else work his shift on the oil rig the night before. I understand now how hard it must have been for them to be pulled in so many directions. Their livelihood, the daily responsibilities of a family and me being so far from home were at odds with each other. No matter how big their "want to" was it couldn't bridge the reality of the distance that lay between us.

Still, every Saturday and Sunday we watched and waited for two solid hours, hoping and praying that our families would come. Our eyes were all fixed on the double swinging doors that open onto the ward. It was as if we were afraid to blink for fear we would miss them. Sometimes they came but, much too often they didn't.

When visiting hours began, it was like a scene from a grand opening at Wal-Mart. There was urgency in our parents' step as if they were running with the bulls in Pamplona, Spain. The parents and children alike knew those two precious hours would go by way too fast.

Heaven help you if your mom decided to change her hair color from the last time you saw her, because it could get confusing for everyone. With our eyes fixed on the distant door, we looked for the features we remembered, features we could recognize. If your mom had blond hair the last time you saw her, and she showed up with red hair the next time, not only would you not see her coming, some other child whose mom had red hair was already waiting with open arms for her to hold him. Someone was going to end up crying no matter who it was that came through the door.

Those parents who came always tried to comfort the children whose parents didn't, but it never was quite the same. The saddest, most dreaded sound we ever heard came over the intercom two days a week, when they would tell us visiting hours were over. Mom cried in a dignified way and Dad cried silently inside his heart and I tried to choke back tears until they left. Most of my crying was reserved for late at night when I prayed. I believe God heard every single prayer and He saw every little tear.

Chasing The Wind

Chapter 4

The Gift

The hospital was broken down into two wards. Ward A was for pre-surgical patients and those who recently underwent a surgical procedure. Ward B was for those who needed rehab and were getting ready for discharge. There were no private rooms, unless you count the isolation room, but that was only used for infectious patients. We slept, ate and cried in beds side by side. There were sixteen-year-old kids with peach fuzz faces and babies with peach bottoms. What a sight we were, but we were a family.

I would average six to eight months of every year in that home away from home and there were many nights I lay awake asking God why. I wrestled with the complexities and mixed emotions of why I had to be there, and then with being thankful that I had found this much needed haven. I needed to know why I was different. Why was this my lot in life, what did I do wrong? Why me Lord? Did my parents not love me? Were they ever coming back for me? Soon there would be a series of events in my life that would lead me to the answers I had been searching for, for so long. It started when six rusty strings met ten little figures of a lonely eight-year-old boy. It was then that the light of God's gift began to shine.

By the time I turned eight years old I had painted, weaved and carved every arts and craft known to modern man. The Occupational Therapist at the hospital was working hard to find something to keep me busy. We would spend one day a week trying to break up the monotony of the other six. There was no way she could have known the change that would take place in my life just by finding that old Silver Tone.

When it was first made, I am sure its maker could not have imagined where it would end up. But, there it was, hidden behind a big stack of teddy bears. This old guitar had been donated to everyone and then forgotten by all. God knew it was there and He gave it to me when I needed it most. My therapist told me I could have it if I could tune it. "Great!" I thought, how hard could that be?

My parents always sent money in my get-well cards, so I could buy new batteries for my transistor radio. It had an ear-piece that was like my umbilical cord to the world outside. I spent hours a day listening to everything from the Beatles to Elvis to Marty Robins. I loved it all.

I had a mission to make that old guitar mine, but first I had to tune it. "How do you do that," I wondered to myself but I didn't have a clue. I knew I had to be able to turn the tuning knobs and for that I needed a rust remover. A Mel Bay guitar book or two wouldn't hurt either.

One day, I asked one of the nurses if she would take some of my money and buy a can of WD-40 for me to use on my "new" rusty guitar. I was focused, excited and alive. After assembling all the tools I would need for the job, I worked tirelessly for three straight days and finally that Silver Tone guitar was mine.

I know now that the therapist and God wouldn't have had it any other way. The tuning of that old guitar mirrored the harmonic changes that were starting to take place in my heart. While I was busy tuning those six strings, God started the process of tuning my life.

I practiced on the old guitar for several hours a day, everyday and over time it slowly began to sound like something more than a rock in a tin can. The idea that God had given me a gift renewed my hope and, for the first time in my life, I began to focus on what I had, instead of what I had lost. I began to see myself in a different light. It was no longer a question of what I couldn't do but rather what I could, and I wanted to show everyone who would listen. That part was easy; after all, I did have a captive audience.

I played my guitar no matter what condition I was in. There were many times I would accidentally pull out IV needles that were placed in my wrist and hands. Realizing I was not going to stop playing, the nurses put the IV fluids in my forearm and the tops of my feet. It made less work for them while giving me the freedom of movement. I was determined to sing and play, no matter what.

Chasing The Wind

Chapter 5

Waiting for the Push

It is amazing how kids can find ways to entertain themselves with limited resources. We had no video games, X-Boxes or Game Cubes. In fact we had only two television sets, one on each side of the ward for all of us to share. But, there was a place known as the "catwalk" located on "Ward A."

A walkway went around the outside of the ward where dignitaries and others we didn't know would walk past and look into the windows of the ward. At times, we felt like we were living in a fish bowl, but we didn't mind. A new face was a new face.

I am not quite sure who came up with the idea, but it was a classic. We would take some of the 50 cc irrigation syringes that were always around someone's bed, and fill them up with water. (For those of you who aren't acquainted with 50cc syringes, they're really big and hold a lot of liquid). We would sneak onto the "cat walk" in our wheelchairs and race head long at each other, squirting all the way.

It was sort of our own medieval games with our wheelchairs for horses. It was fun while it lasted but the mess it caused put an end to the games. The nursing staff was always forgiving, because, I think they must have known what we were going through.

Physical therapy was the thing we needed most each day, and it was also the thing we dreaded most. Not because of the staff but because of the pain. If you went to PT, there was going to be some pain. They were dedicated to getting the best out of you and you were going to give it one way or another. Not only would they work on strengthening weak muscles and increasing range of motion and the simple complexities of how to walk, they also taught us how to fall. Because of the condition most of us were in, they knew we were going to fall somewhere, sometime. It was best if we knew how to do it in a way that limited the damage and the pain.

The therapist would put us on a cushioned mat and take away our crutches or walker and proceed to push us over. To the untrained eye, I'm sure it looked cruel and it seemed that way to us at times, too. Most of the injuries that happen in a fall are caused because you panic. We had to learn to face our fear. We were pushed from the left and then the right, from the front and from behind. The anticipation of waiting for 'the push' was infuriating. As we got older, we got over the fear and it became a game.

This lesson has served me well over the years. Life comes at you in so many unexpected directions, often running you down or hitting you from your blind spot. You lay on the ground saying to yourself, "Not again! I have had enough." The point is not the number of times in your life you get knocked down but how you get back up.

This exercise has a spiritual meaning to me as well. When you fall, and we're all going to fall from time to time in our lives, you'll find it doesn't hurt as much if you know where to fall. The softest place I've found is into the arms of Jesus.

William Boyd Chisum

Chasing The Wind

Chapter 6

The Island of Misfit Toys

Keeping up with our education while in the hospital was always difficult. I had a tutor who came twice a week to give me new assignments and check my homework. There was only one dear lady to teach all of the school age children at the hospital. She was soft spoken with a calming presence about her and, at times, the daunting task of teaching us overwhelmed her. What a ministry she took on as she tried to educate all of us and give us hope for a brighter future. I am not sure any of us looked that far ahead. We couldn't even see tomorrow's sunrise from where we were.

Holidays were hard for those of us that weren't able to go home. Christmas was the hardest to get through. I can remember one Christmas Eve when the nurse came and put me in a wheelchair so she could take me out to the nurse's desk to take a phone call from my parents. They were not going to be able to come for the holidays and had called to wish me a Merry Christmas. I put on a stiff upper lip and acted like I was fine with it, but inside I was devastated.

After the phone call ended, I stayed out by the nurse's desk and we all sang Christmas carols together. There were only a handful of children left in the hospital by that time. The others were lucky enough to go home for the holiday.

On Christmas morning a group of people, I didn't know nor had ever seen before, came in and loaded my hospital bed full of presents and all the gifts had my name on them. Even though I was not at home, somehow Santa had found me. I was not a "misfit from the island of misfit toys" after all. More important than all the presents, was the fact that I had been remembered. It was a Christmas I have never forgotten.

William Boyd Chisum

Chasing The Wind

Chapter 7

Unleashed "Puppy Love"

One of the benefits of being on Ward B was that we could go down to the auditorium to watch a movie on Friday nights. Those who could walk or ride in a wheelchair were loaded up and sent down the long hallway that ran between the admissions desk and Ward A. However, if we were unable to ambulate or otherwise leave our bed, the nurses would roll us down to the auditorium, bed and all.

The winding trail of happy children reminded me of a carnival parade filled with pulse-pounding excitement. It was also an opportunity for the boys to meet and visit with the girls of Ward B. Anyone who was there would tell you that, from time to time, "puppy love" ran unleashed down the halls of Scottish Rite Hospital, especially on Friday night at the movies.

We had an in-house weekly newspaper called the "Scotty." It allowed us to read about the new kids who had been admitted as well as write encouraging notes to one another. Every week they would pass out little square pieces of paper for us to write a note on or draw a picture and then they would print your masterpiece in the weekly paper. It was just a chance to express how you felt and to make new friends. It was a tool for us to get outside ourselves, forget our own situation and connect with others who might have a need.

Chasing The Wind

Chapter 8

Keith

Have you ever met someone that you know in your heart you will never forget? I grew up with several of those kinds of people. There was a little boy whose name was Keith. He was several years younger than me, but I admired him immensely. Keith had a smile that would light up the whole ward and gave little indication to the trauma his young life had already experienced.

Keith had been run over by a train and had lost both legs, one arm at the elbow and all the fingers except one on the remaining hand. He was left with only a small stub for a thumb. Never once in all the months that we were there together did I hear him complain. He always had the biggest smile on his face and just seemed to be happy to be alive.

Keith was the first person, I can recall, to show me that anything is possible. He was a natural when it came to walking on his prosthetic limbs. He not only made it look easy, but soon he was running around chasing those of us who were wheelchair bound. Keep in mind this was long before the space age, high tech material that they make limbs from today. No arms and no legs, but if Keith had a single care in the world, he never showed it. It made us all ashamed when we began to feel sorry for ourselves.

Little Keith was so excited because the doctors were going to build him an index finger to go with the stub he had for a thumb because then he could go to school. Just to be able to hold a pencil and write was all he wanted. I watched as God used those doctors to create a miracle in his life. It took a year, but when I saw him leave, he had an index finger and he could write his name.

His body was far from perfect in the eyes of most people in the world, but God must have said, "This is someone I can use to inspire others," and I have no doubt that, in God's eyes, Keith was perfect. In times of need, God provides strength in places and people we least expect. For me, at that time in my life, it came in the face of a little boy who had a smile as big as his courage and his name was Keith.

Chapter 9

My Grand Canyon

Did you ever want something so much, that the thought of it beat like a drum in your mind, day in and day out? But, when that dream finally came true, you were left with a sense of let down?

I lay in bed countless nights longing to go home but when my dream would eventually come true, I found that there were difficult family adjustments and reconnections that had to be made. My brother, who from time to time each year went from being an only child to being older brother, then back again, had to learn how to share his mom and dad with someone he hardly knew and could not relate to anymore.

I am sure the attention I received was met with a sense of jealousy and misunderstanding. There had to be comfort in knowing his life would return to normal as soon as I returned to my 'other' home. This natural yo-yo of emotions for him and me would leave a chasm in our relationship too wide for either of us to cross.

The bond between a child and his parents is a strong one and can rarely be broken, no matter what. That bond can, however, be reshaped and have its warm and fuzziness weathered away like wind and rain reshapes boulders on the side of a weather-beaten mountain.

The erosion takes place slowly, almost unseen over time, but the demands can become so great that it forces you to move prematurely from a relationship of paternal and maternal love into a relationship of mutual respect. If I have learned one thing, it's that absence does not necessarily make the heart grow fonder, but it will inevitably make it grow stronger.

William Boyd Chisum

Chasing The Wind

Chapter 10

Solitaire

I was back at home once again and my mother had made a bed on a cot in the living room so I could watch my brother, James, and the neighbor's children playing in the yard. For the first time in a long time I was not in a body cast and could sit up and look at the world outside. I had graduated to a pair of crutches and, although I wanted so much to go outside and play with the other kids, I couldn't. Not yet.

There were children in every home that surrounded the little house where my family now lived. It was not unusual for my parents to move to a new town or location while I was in the hospital, and that added to the apprehension as well as the excitement of going home. What would it look like? Would there be other children in the neighborhood for me to get to know? As I listened to Jan, Brenda, Kenneth and Ronnie Penter from the house next door play baseball with my brother in our front yard it seemed I was in a foreign country. I had not heard children's laughter like that in a long time and I was happy to be home.

My new home had a dark brick exterior and was nestled back off the road with several tall pine trees in the front yard. The driveway sloped away from the main road in a steep grade. The front yard was full of green grass, enough to keep my brother busy mowing it all summer long. Our simple, modest two-bedroom home was in a fairly new subdivision, located in a sleepy little town called Wake Village, just outside of Texarkana, Texas.

The backyard led into the thickest piney woods I had ever seen. The honeysuckle vines that were the dividing line between our yard and a world of imagination gave off a sweet, almost heavenly, fragrance, which drifted on the breeze. It was such a refreshing change from the sterile antiseptic world I was accustomed to.

The daily sounds of rattling wheels from dinner carts, mop buckets and wheelchairs were replaced with gentle winds blowing through the tall pines and blue jays squawking in the fig tree by the well house out back. My senses were overwhelmed as I began to enjoy the freedom of this new life.

I had been home for a couple of weeks when I started noticing the change. I tried to keep it to myself and pretend it wasn't happening, and hoped maybe the red streaks running up and down my hip would just go away. I had not been here long enough, and I couldn't bear the thought of having to leave. I was successful in keeping it from my parents for only a few days. But then, my fever flushed cheeks and sweat-soaked bed linens, which I could no longer hide, gave me away.

I had developed an infection deep down in my hip joint. By the time my parents were aware of the infection; my left hip had already begun to swell and was hot to the touch. I knew in my heart what had to happen, long before my father put in a call to the doctors at Scottish Rite. I was going back.

There I was, lying on an exam table at a medical clinic in Texarkana, waiting to confirm what everyone was already thinking. I had a staff infection of the left hip and the test they were about to do would substantiate that fact. When my father talked to the doctors at Scottish Rite, they advised him to take me to the clinic in

Texarkana and have a culture done on the fluid inside my hip joint. The clinic was to send the test results to Dallas so a plan of action could be determined.

If the white cell count was not too high, maybe there was still a chance that oral antibiotics could put a stop to the infection before surgical intervention would be necessary.

I couldn't remember ever having an aspiration done before so I was a little afraid of the process. It just didn't sound like fun to me. As the clinic doctor sterilized the hip for the procedure, my father tried to slip away.

It wasn't just that he hated needles. It was more the fact he could not stand to watch someone he loved be in pain. However, I was prepared for his departure and quickly grabbed his hand. I was determined not to let go. Whatever was coming I knew I could take it better if I was holding his hand.

When everyone was ready, a large gauge needle was inserted into my hip until it reached the inside of the socket. I gritted my teeth, trying to hold my breath along with the scream that wanted so desperately to escape from my mouth. The plunger on the syringe was then pulled back, filling it with a dirty thick brown fluid.

I looked up at my father whose hand was now turning white from my grip on it, and I saw a tear slowly roll down his cheeks. This was an earth-shattering revelation to me. In all we had been through, I had never seen him cry. It was then that I began to see how much all of this was hurting him. I never realized how helpless he must have felt, sitting on the sidelines wishing he could take my place.

My dad could not take my place that day or any other, so he did the only thing he could do. He drove me back to the hospital in Dallas to be admitted.

The test showed I had a staff infection in my left hip and oral antibiotics were not going to be an option. I was going to need massive amounts of IV medication along with surgery to open up the hip and let it drain. All of this would take place in the only private room available on Ward A, and that meant isolation.

After being admitted, I was escorted by one of the nurses from Ward A to a large bathroom. She filled a tub with water and asked me to bathe using an antimicrobial liquid. It was very important when I went into the isolation room that I take as few germs with me as possible. The nurse then told me where I could find a gown, washcloth and towels.

She left me with my thoughts and a churning in my stomach that I knew was due to nerves. I placed my crutches against the wall at the head of the tub and slid into the warm water. I was so upset about being back at the hospital again so soon and facing the unknown that I began to feel the loss of control of my bowels. It happened so fast I could not get up and out of the bath. What strength I had, was suddenly gone and I felt helpless and humiliated. Panic began to set in as I tried to get out of the mess I had made in the tub.

If I could just clean it up then no one would know. I grabbed towels and washcloths and the more I worked to hide my shame the worse it became. I was so afraid I was going to be in trouble and that maybe the nurses would think I was just too lazy to get out of the tub. Then I heard a knock on the bathroom door and the nurse asking me if I was almost done with my bath. Fear ran through me like a bolt of electricity. I could not let her see me this way.

I asked for a few more minutes but I think the tone in my voice gave me away. She opened the door and gasped when she saw me on my hands and knees scooping up the mess I had made. In my panic to clean up the tub, I had given little thought to what I looked like and how I was covered from head to toe.

When I realized I had been seen, I lay down on the cold tile floor and began to cry. I never felt more alone in my life as I did in that moment. I cried out over and over that it was an accident and that I was sorry. The nurse bent down and covered me with a clean towel, attempting to console me. She was gentle, warm and understanding as she worked to clean me up. My world had fallen apart and I felt lost and alone. No amount of cleaning that night was going to wash that feeling away.

Lying on my bed in the isolation room, I could see the increase of activity around the nurses' desk. I knew everyone was helping with the cleanup and I expected to hear comments for days to come, but I never heard a single word from anyone.

Isn't it amazing how God does the same thing in our life when we come to know Him? He finds us wallowing in our sin, coated in the filth of this world with nothing to hide us, and still, He reaches out in love and cleans us up and remembers our sin no more. Thank you Lord for that living lesson which You gave me.

The isolation room was like being in solitary confinement. Everyone who came into my room had to put on a sterile gown and gloves and a mask for protection. These precautions were more for my protection than theirs. So there I was waiting for the next shoe to drop, and I didn't have to wait very long.

I was put on IV antibiotics and had a heating pad on my hip around the clock. I did not understand how hot moist heat was going to help this condition. How in the world would that make anything better? I was going to find out real soon. They weren't trying to make it better; they were trying to bring the infection to the surface. Once that happened, it would be easier to clean it out and then try to keep it clean. The big question I had was, easier for whom?

The whole process of cooking the germs to a boil took a couple days. When the infection began to ooze out of my skin, like blisters popping from a sunburn, the doctors realized they had waited too long to take me to surgery for what is simply called an 'incision and drainage.'

At this point, they could not risk rolling me down the halls of the hospital to surgery, spreading my bacteria like a city sprays for mosquitoes. No, the procedure would have to be done in my Isolation room and without the benefits of anesthesia. The next shoe had just dropped.

The betadine scrub the doctor was using to prep my hip for surgery was cold and thick and was a rusty yellow color. Using 4x4 gauzes and a pair of hemostats, the betadine was applied in small circular movements from the center of the hip moving outward.

I thought of the irony of spending so much effort to sterilize the surface of an area, when what lay underneath was so contaminated. The doctor then injected a local anesthetic into my hip to make the procedure easier for me to endure. Without any advance warning, with scalpel in hand, a circular incision was made down to the hip socket.

I chewed on the corner of my pillowcase expecting the worst, but it was over in just a matter of seconds. The combination of my adrenaline, the injection and the speed of the scalpel, not to mention the fact that the infection had turned my underlying muscle to liquid, made what I feared would be horrible, tolerable.

I was asked to roll over onto a basin to allow the infection to pour out. The wound was then cleaned and irrigated and left open in order for the healing process to begin from the inside out, a process that would take several months.

As the days turned to weeks and weeks to months, I would not feel the touch of another human hand, unless it had a glove on it. It was at night, when the lights were turned out, that I longed to be held in my mother's arms. Even though I knew every inch of my room by heart, in the darkness of the night, I needed my dad's strong hands to chase away my fears and protect me from the unknown.

Chasing The Wind

Chapter  11

Red Light/Green Light

Everything that I took with me into the isolation room would have to stay in that room until all of the infection was gone. The only thing I really cared about having was my guitar. If I could play and sing, I knew I could get through this.

It was inside my music that I found the ability to escape, and I would need to do that here more than I ever had before. A duet a day, performed by my music and imagination would lead me to freedom from this twenty by fifteen foot room they called isolation.

I made up songs about the doctors. I made up songs about my nurses, too. In isolation I felt secure in giving it my all when I sang. No one could hear me so I just "opened up my mouth and let God out." Those four walls that I had become so accustomed to looking at did not intimidate me one bit. I wasn't afraid to sing to them. They couldn't tell others what they heard. Or could they? Well, that's what I thought anyway.

Somehow, the concept of time was something I didn't worry about. I kept track of time by when my meals were served. It was early in the evening, I think. We had already been served dinner from the dinner cart and the trays had been picked up by the nursing staff.

Anyway, it was time for my nightly four-wall concert and as I strummed and sang, it all came from my heart. It didn't occur to me that the nursing staff had the ability to turn on the intercom system in my room. Nor could I have imagined they would be sneaky enough to broadcast it to all of the rooms on Ward A. But there it was, the distinct echo of my voice coming from outside my room.

Yes, my voice was being amplified to the nurses' desk. But how? On the wall behind my head was the call light system that allowed me to call if I needed assistance. There were two lights on the control panel, red and green. The green light meant I wanted to talk to someone at the desk and red light indicated they were listening. There it was, shining brighter than Rudolph's nose and right under my own nose too. The red light was on and the faint sound of giggling told me it had been for quite awhile.

The cheers and applause from the nursing staff did little to ease my embarrassment. The concert was over for the night and I would have to be more careful in the future.

I thought I had it all under control once I realized that I needed to keep an eye on the red light indicator. When it came on, I would simply stop singing and playing. It worked well for a few days until one of the nurses boldly walked into my room, gowned up and put on her mask and gloves, and then calmly walked over to the head of my bed and pulled out the bulb on the wall that went to the red light. "Now you won't know if we're listening or not," she said with a laugh. I guess I was forced to get over my butterflies of performing in front of people by those inventive and loving nurses on Ward A.

Scottish Rite Hospital would at times have very special guests show up to either tour the facilities or to visit with the children. Everyone from famous sports figures to TV and movie personalities came. To have the ability to get an autograph or a picture taken with any of them made for big topics of conversation for the months to come. It was always one of the first things brought up when meeting a newly admitted child. "Oh by the way, have I shown you the picture I had made with John Wayne last month?" we would ask. It made everyone who was blessed enough to participate have something of pride to hold on to.

There were at least two occasions I was not counted in that group of lucky ones to get autographs or pictures. Not because I wasn't there, oh I was, but because isolation was a place few entered. It was just safer for all the other children on the ward. I did, however, get to wave at the stars as they hurried by, in a big throng of photographers. At least I could say I saw them. Harvey Corman from the Carol Burnett show was one of the nicest of all the ones I met. I could tell if they really wanted to be there, I guess we all could tell, and it was obvious Mr. Corman wanted to make us happy.

I had been in isolation for several months and was beginning to go stir crazy. Did you know that if you looked hard enough and long enough you could count all the little holes in the ceiling tile of your room? I also learned that if you practiced long enough with a rubber band you could "pick off" a toy army man on the windowsill from across the room. These were important things to learn, I thought, and would surely aid me in any career I would choose in the future. It just goes to show it didn't take much to keep me entertained.

The day I had healed enough to leave isolation was a day I will never forget. The nurses came in and for the first time left the door open. They didn't put on sterile gowns, masks or gloves. They just walked straight over and said, "Let's get you out of here." I was going to Ward B.

While the staff started gathering up and cleaning all the belongings I had accumulated over these months, a nurse placed me in a wheelchair for a special surprise that she had planned for me.

Down the long hallway that connected Ward A to Ward B, past the picture of the Scottie dressed in a kilt and cap. I was pushed past the information desk and out the front door onto the circle drive. She rolled my chair over to the sidewalk and put on the brake and allowed me to sit and soak up the outside world for a while. The sun was bright and, even though it was early morning, the humidity of Dallas in the summertime made the air thick and heavy. It was as if I were seeing and feeling and hearing the world for the first time. All things were new and I soaked it in for as long as I could. My skin was pale from being inside for so long, so I could only stay outside for a few minutes. It was the most beautiful day God had ever made and I was sure he made that day just for me.

I watched the squirrels playing under the trees in front of the hospital. I saw cars coming and going from the circle drive by the statue of the nurse holding the child that I loved so much. Life was good again. I knew any moment my nurse would unlock the chair and take me back inside, but I didn't care. Being outside gave me my second wind and I was ready to face life on Ward B, and grateful that this nurse cared enough to show me that the sun could shine on me again.

William Boyd Chisum

Chasing The Wind

Chapter 12

My First Best Friend

There was a section on Ward B that everyone called "the porch." It was a room separated from the others by a single wall with no doors and it opened onto a long narrow space over looking a wall of windows. The hospital used the porch as an overflow when bed space on Ward B was too crowded. There was enough room for five or six beds, side by side, and I am sure it was not due to over-crowding that found me residing on the porch. Could it have been my propensity to play the guitar at all hours of the day and night? Nonetheless, I was glad to be here and, with all the windows where I could look outside, it gave me a feeling of freedom. What a pleasant difference from what I had grown accustomed to.

I was the only person on the porch for several days until a boy by the name of Chris joined me. He was older than I by a couple of years but, in short order, we became best friends. Wherever the nurses saw one of us, they knew the other was soon to follow. Chris had played the trumpet at his junior high school marching band. Music became the bond that brought and held our friendship together.

It wasn't too long before we convinced Chris' parents to bring his trumpet up so we could play together. Within the first few seconds of our first rehearsal, I know without a doubt, that the staff on Ward B had to be thankful they had put us both out on the porch.

Chris was from Henderson, Texas. A farm boy with experiences I had never known. He worked on his grandfather's farm, drove a tractor, bailed hay, all the things I had never done before. Chris was just a normal kid until the day of the accident. He had been on his grandfather's tractor mowing with a brush hog.

For those of you unfamiliar with the term, a brush hog is an attachment on the back of a tractor, usually owned by a city or county, and is used to mow down tall grass on the sides of the roadway. Chris had been mowing a field of tall weeds and grass when he ran over a hive of bees on the ground. As they swarmed up around him, he jumped from the tractor to get away from the constant stinging.

He had tried to turn off the ignition key as he jumped free from the tractor but failed to do so. It was when he tried to crawl back on the tractor that it happened. The large rear wheel ran over him, pulling him down and under the brush hog. He told me it happened so fast. The blades of the brush hog had amputated his left leg above the knee and had taken off his right kneecap. He lay there stunned and in shock until his grandfather noticed the riderless tractor and had run to find him. He was airlifted to a local hospital and, at some point, was transferred to Scottish Rite for surgical reshaping of the amputated stump.

Chris used a mute in the end of his trumpet to lower the volume of our music. Herb Albert and the Tijuana Brass were typical examples of the type of music we played. It was great to be best friends with someone who loved music as much as I had grown to love it. We both listened to our radios around the clock, trying to find new songs to play. We even entered a local radio contest in which the object was to keep track of all the songs that were played and the order they came in.

For twenty-four hours a day we slept in shifts with one of us always having the earpiece to a transistor radio stuck in our ear and pen and paper nearby. We didn't win the contest, so obviously one of us went to sleep at some point. We did not care because we had heard our name on the radio.

Someone on the nursing staff had called the radio station to inform them of our escapades and just how dedicated a fan base they had in us. The DJ's from that moment on rarely failed to say hello to us while on the air. We were stars at last.

When Chris left me on the porch to go home, it was a great day for him but sad one for me. He had received a prosthetic left leg and a brace for the right one. He was going home to the farm and back to school with his friends. Life for him was going to get better, just as he had made my life better over those months that we shared together. He was my first best friend and I would miss him a lot.

Not all the kids that I met were like Chris. Some had become bitter and mean over the hand that life had dealt them. It was easy to understand how that could happen, having seen what so many of the children there had to deal with. But I was not prepared to handle what would take place between me and a sixteen-year-old young man.

We were on a collision course, and nothing could have stopped what was about to take place. Up to this point, I had experienced a life filled with love and friendship. I had not been exposed to the evil or the down right meanness that a human being could harbor in his heart or inflict on someone else. I was about to see a close up example of both.

Chasing The Wind

Chapter 13

Living on Hate

It is not my intent in the writing of this book to paint anyone in a way that would damage or hurt their character. It is, however, my intent to tell the truth. With that in mind, I will not use the real name of that sixteen-year-old boy. For all I know, perhaps he has changed and asked for forgiveness for the things I am about to tell. I can only pray that God has made a difference in his life and altered the path down which he was obviously headed.

At no time have I ever believed that anyone, other than the children on Ward B, knew what was going on in the dark of night. I am certain that, had anyone of us had the courage to speak out about what was happening, the hospital staff would have moved heaven and earth to protect us.

'Johnny' had issues in his life that none of us could understand. In all the time he spent in the hospital we never saw anyone come to visit him. Did he not have family or did they not love him? We never knew. But what we did know caused us to be afraid of this older boy with long hair and a hairy chin.

Johnny had been pierced in the side by a shotgun and it damaged his spine. We never knew who it was that shot him and the circumstances surrounding the shooting was a topic of wild speculation. I don't think any us ever knew the real story. But it was obvious to all of us, including the staff, that Johnny was an angry young man.

He was a big kid -- tall and muscular with long arms that you wanted to stay away from. The shotgun blast had destroyed some of the vertebrae in his spine and, after several surgeries, he had been placed in skeletal traction. He had pins drilled into his skull that were attached to an orthopedic halo. A rope ran from the halo through a pulley and over the head of his bed to weights that helped pull his spine out straight.

He also had a similar setup for both legs at the knees. This pulled his spine in opposite directions allowing healing to take place over time. He was bedridden, miserable, and hated everyone for it. Time could not move fast enough for Johnny and everyone on the ward was caught up in the ticking time bomb that was his life.

On Ward B, all the beds were side by side and we had little to no control over who was on either side of us. No one wanted to be next to Johnny but someone had to be. I guess they thought it best to put younger children on both sides, probably believing Johnny would have less of an issue with younger children than those of us closer to his age.

There was a little boy in the bed to the right of Johnny who had a problem with soiling his pants at night. With every accident, Johnny would try to scare the boy into not doing it again. He told all of us who would listen that if it were the last thing he did, he would make this little boy stop messing on himself. We never thought much about his threats because he could not get up to get to the little boy. We were wrong in thinking Johnny had to get up to get to him and what happened late that night changed a lot of us forever.

I was awakened by the sound of Johnny cursing at the little boy in the bed to his right. From what I could make out from their conversation and harsh words through clinched teeth, the little boy had another accident in his pants and Johnny could smell it. He was furious and was belittling the boy unmercifully.

Suddenly I could hear in the darkness the sound of a bed being moved and the whimpers of a little boy. Someone had left the beds too close together that day and Johnny had reached out with one of his long arms and pulled the little boy's bed next to his. I heard the metal sound of the bed rail going down and knew instantly what was taking place. Johnny had his hands on that little boy and was fulfilling his promise to teach him a lesson.

I lowered my bed rail and reached for my crutches. When I crossed the isle to the other side of the room I was horrified at what I saw. Johnny had removed the dirty shorts of the little boy and was proceeding to rub his face in it. I demanded that he stop and let the little boy go, but all he said was what are you going to do about it? And he was right, what could I do about it? I knew I could not risk getting too close to his powerful arms.

The safest place for me was at the end of his bed, but how could I stop all of this from the end of his bed? The only things other than me at the foot of his bed were the weights that hung from the pins in his knees. Then it hit me. I reached out and slapped the weights making them swing, causing the pins to move in his knees. I got his attention, but all he did was curse me and tell me what he would to do to me if he could get his hands on me.

I begged him to let the boy go but he acted like he didn't hear me. He proceeded to torment the little boy on and on. I finally reached out and picked up the weights and dropped them over and over, until he couldn't stand it any more and he let go of the child and cried out in pain. One of the other children grabbed the little boy's bed from the opposite side and pulled it out of Johnny's reach.

By this time the eleven-to-seven nursing staff was marching in with their little pin lights waving in the air wanting to know what was going on. One of their flashlights focused on the little boy who Johnny had forced to eat his own feces. He was whimpering and choking. I felt numb and nauseous and could not understand how someone could be so cruel.

The next morning Johnny was moved from Ward B and we never saw him again. We didn't ask where he went, we were just glad he was gone. That was the first time I can remember intentionally hurting another human being. I fully expected to be in trouble over what I had done to Johnny but, if administration or the staff knew, they never mentioned it to me.

I think dealing with a loss of something in your life like your mobility or an arm or leg is harder for those who can remember what it was like to be whole. I guess I was one of the fortunate one's because what I had, what I was living with every day, was all I had ever known. It must be easier for those of us who fantasize over what has never been than for those who sadly remember what once was.

William Boyd Chisum

Chasing The Wind

Chapter 14

It Is I, Be Not Afraid

Anesthesia was a part of surgery that I did not look forward to. Ether was the drug of choice for many years and it always left me nauseated and with a severe headache. I had to even undergo anesthesia every time I was placed into a body cast. They had to maneuver my legs into a position that stretched some of the tendons far beyond what I was able to endure while awake. When the resistance of the tendons caused the hips to fall short of the position they needed to be in, a scalpel was used to help tear the tendon into submission. The tendons on the inner thigh at the groin were usually the ones that would end up impaled and forced to stretch past their capabilities.

I was somewhere around eleven years old when they finally came up with a new drug for anesthesia. I was unaware of this new discovery, however, until I was lying on the table waiting to be put under. As they placed the oxygen mask over my face, I felt a cold sensation moving up my arm and across my chest. The intravenous medication was quickly working itself through my body. Suddenly my whole body seized up as if it were in the throws of one giant muscle spasm. I was paralyzed and could not breathe or move any part of my body. I was awake but unable to speak. My eyes were fixated in one position. I knew I was in trouble by the panic I heard from each voice in the room. I sensed that everyone was hurrying around trying to undue this allergic reaction I was having to this new anesthesia. It is an awful feeling to know you are suffocating to death and you can't move or scream. In the midst of all the confusion, I heard a nurse accidentally turn over a tray of instruments and the sound of them hitting the floor echoed in my ears. Suddenly the panic in my brain turned to peace, and I was inexplicably calm. I felt completely at rest as I slipped into the darkness. It was as if I heard a voice calling to me saying "It is I, be not afraid." Since that day I have faced the possibility of death with a calm assurance. I know without a doubt who and what awaits me on the other side of the "valley of the shadow of death" and that knowledge fills me with a "peace that passes all understanding."

William Boyd Chisum

Chasing The Wind

Chapter 15

The Great Escape

I had been in the hospital for almost a year straight and was expecting to get to go home soon, when I was told that the plans had changed. They were going to try a new procedure called a cup arthroplasty and my discharge was going to have to wait. I could not believe it. I was angry and feeling sorry for myself when I told Mr. Henderson, the male nurse who broke the bad news, that if they did not let me go home I would leave on my own accord.

He strongly advised me not to do anything rash or stupid. I promised him I would find a way out if he didn't help me. He said he would put in a call to see what could be done. It didn't sound promising to me so I began looking for a way to escape.

After the lights went out that night on Ward B, I waited until the nurses made their rounds. I was in the bed against the far wall at the end of Ward B, which meant I was next to a window. The windows were made in two parts. They had a crank, similar to those on some mobile homes, with which to open the windows. I was able to pull myself through the open window and out, onto the walkway below.

It was a cool night and the circle drive seemed to be wet as if it had rained. If it had, it wasn't a hard or steady rain or I would have noticed while waiting for the nurse to make her final rounds. I reached back in through the window and grabbed my crutches and then set out on a walk to an unknown destination.

I tried to be careful, hoping not to be noticed. But being stealthy on crutches was impossible, so I walked as slowly as I could and tried to stay in the shadows, all the time wondering where I was going. I had a bunch of questions for which I had no answers. There was only one thing I was sure of, I was fed up with this place and I needed a break.

Here I was running away from home, by trying to get home. Just the thought was confusing enough for me to have stayed where I was, but I ended up doing exactly what Mr. Henderson had asked me not to do, something stupid.

I did not get very far until the security guard spotted me. I can't imagine what gave me away. Was it the tips of my crutches making a suction sound against the wet pavement or the fact that I was breathing so hard that the condensation of my breath must have looked like a smoke stack on a coal train. Whatever the reason, on my crutches, I could not out run the security guard. So after a short therapeutic excursion into the night, I was brought back.

Mr. Henderson was furious with me. He asked if I understood all the bad things that could have happened to me, and of course I didn't. I didn't know and didn't care. I just wanted to go home. He sent me back to Ward B and made me promise to wait while he made a few phone calls.

I guess he received the clearance from the doctors for me to get a week-long pass, but my parents could not come and get me. My dad was in the Border Patrol academy at the time and could not get away. Dad made a call to my grandmother's house and a plan slowly took shape. My Aunt Helen and two of her sisters, Murle and Lois, would accompany my grandmother to come for me. Aunt Maloise had major dental surgery that day, and was not in good shape to travel. But, my aunts made a pallet in the back of the station wagon for her, loaded up and headed out to Dallas. I was going to get a much-needed break.

I enjoyed that week with my aunts and cousins but it all went by way too fast. I can remember walking out onto the front porch of Aunt Helen's house each morning and being in awe of the amount of dew that had collected on the grass over night. It was the little things in life that most people had become accustomed to and didn't notice anymore that I found amazing and new. I was thankful to be here and thankful for a family that cared enough to come and rescue me from the foolish actions of a lonely boy. Seven days later I was back at Ward A, waiting for another round of surgeries.

Chasing The Wind

Chapter 16

Words Unspoken

Time marches on even when things around us seem to be at a standstill. I was getting close to fourteen and had been through isolation three more times due to the failed attempts of the cup arthroplasties. I kept coming down with staff infection in my left hip. The doctors tried everything but the results were always the same.

A phone call was made to the man who pioneered the surgery, Dr. Head, and he agreed to come to Dallas and perform the procedure himself. The fourth try was a success and the light I began to see at the end of the tunnel, for the first time in my life, was not a train. What would be the final round for me on Ward B was a time of sheer joy.

I had friends around me and for the first time I was the oldest boy there. I was able to pass on a few of the old tricks I learned to a group of young and eager kids. Tricks like how to pop wheelies in a wheelchair and not fall over backwards and dislocate your hip. I had a personal experience with that one.

It was a wonderful time in my life. I was able to mentor and be a big brother to the little kids who needed someone to show them the way, and how to face the things that scared them the most. I told them the story of what a doctor told me about how not to cry in front of the other kids. I explained how to keep it to yourself, how to hold it in so you wouldn't upset the younger kids. Learning how to stuff your emotions was rule number one on the list. These were the things I learned from my peers. It would take years for me to unlearn some of those lessons. Even in the writing of these pages I have had to dig down deep to express the true emotions and feelings that have for so long been buried.

I also tried to help them understand that they needed to watch out for the little ones and take care of each other. I had learned that when I concentrated on the needs of the younger kids I did not think of myself so much. I needed to pass this on to them before I left.

It began to look like I would be going home soon. I was up, walking on my crutches, feeling great without a care in the world. If I had one you wouldn't have known it. I had learned that one from my friend Keith.

I had been told that once I regained my strength and mobility I could progress from crutches to two canes. I was so excited because I would finally get to go home and start public school. What would it feel like to go to class, sit in a desk and do all the things fourteen-year-old kids do? I wanted to find out.

The day finally arrived when I was released from Scottish Rite Hospital for good. I would still have to come in for yearly check ups over the next two years, but I would never again be admitted as a patient. On that fateful day my father drove up from a small town in south Texas called Carrizo Springs. He was now working for the Immigration and Naturalization Service and was stationed close to the Texas/Mexico border.

Mom stayed home to plan a welcome home party for me. As I sat, anxiously waiting to be discharged, I felt I could not leave this place without trying to find Dr. Carrell. This man either performed himself or directed others in every surgery I had undergone for fourteen years. I could not leave without seeing him one more time.

With discharge papers in hand, ready to leave one home for another, I stood in front of the elevators that would take me to the doctor's lunchroom in the basement. I had asked the nurses where I could find Dr. Carrell and that was their best guess.

I rode the elevator down and wondered what I would say to this man. I practiced my lines in my head because I wanted him to remember me as I knew I would always remember him. I walked off the elevator and looked into the lunchroom. There were a lot of white lab coats in there that day, but it didn't take long for my eyes to find him. His black hair, now streaked with gray and smoke emanating from his pipe, made a combination that was hard if not impossible to miss.

I walked over to his table, all the while going over the eloquent words I had planned to say. When he noticed me, Dr. Carrell stood up to shake my hand and all my plans and speeches went out the window. I looked at him with his big smile and piercing blue eyes and all I could say was "goodbye" and "thank you." My eyes never left his and I hope he understood that there was so much more I wanted to say.

The same heart that was jumping for joy to be going home was breaking all at the same time. I knew I would never be a patient here again. I knew I would miss the sounds, the smells, the staff, I had grown to love. I was walking out into a whole new world and yet I was leaving so much of me here, at Scottish Rite Hospital.

All that I had, I owed to God, the strength of my parents, the hands of gifted surgeons like Dr. Brandon Carrell and the staff at Texas Scottish Rite Hospital for Children.

As I walked out to the circular driveway, I could see my dad in the distance, his car inching closer to pick me up. My mind was still stuck on my short conversation with Dr. Carrell, wishing I had said more. Dad helped me into the car and we drove away as I looked through the back window, the hospital fading into the distance.

As we drove out of Dallas on Interstate 35 headed for San Antonio and then on to Carrizo Springs, I was nervous about what my life would be like. How would I fit in? Would I be able to make friends? I didn't have the answers to any of the questions rolling in my mind, but I knew without a doubt, that the past I was leaving behind had prepared me for what lay ahead.

William Boyd Chisum

Chasing The Wind

Chapter 17

"For Gods Sake, Ring the Bell"

I was finally home. Each new day found me struggling to regain my strength and mobility from the last cup arthroplasty procedure. I still had an open wound on my left hip that had to be cleaned and bandaged in addition to daily physical therapy. Every night just like clock work, Mom was there with 4x4 gauze pads, peroxide and Q-tips. She poured the peroxide into the hip until it began to bubble all the necrotizing tissue to the surface and she would then use the Q-tips to clean out the wound. The hole in my hip was the size of a golf ball and ran deep. So deep in fact, you could see the metal cup implanted in my hip for a socket. Mom was always amazed that she could see her own reflection from the stainless steel metal cup as she peered inside. This nightly process was not for the faint of heart, but then neither was the physical therapy that would soon follow. Somehow my mother always found the strength to do what was needed.

My physical therapy consisted of strengthening, range of motion and stretching exercises. My abductor muscles had been cut through so many times in thirteen and a half years, they were virtually nonexistent. I didn't even have the muscle strength to do a lateral leg raise without the help of someone else. Mom would mysteriously turn into the "big bad" physical therapist each and every night when the sun went down.

It was a time that neither of us ever enjoyed, and one from which the rest of the family could not easily escape. Our living room floor became the nightly torture chamber.

Each time before bed I would plead with my mom to forget my therapy for the night but she was always consistent if not persistent. She would make me lie on the floor and she would start with the stretching exercises. The thing about stretching extremities full of scar tissue is that you receive no benefit from it at all unless you push it past the point of pain. It's at that point where all the scar tissue and adhesions are being stretched and torn away so that over time you will have more mobility. The pain from the stretching and tearing of the scar tissue was incredible. A burning sensation shot down my legs like I was set on fire. My muscles would twitch and spasm like they were dancing to music that only they could hear. Just when I would think it was almost over, when I was just about to catch my breath, Mom would push again past the previous point leaving me flailing my arms against the floor like a referee counting out a wrestler on a mat. I waited for someone to ring the bell for this mother and child wrestling match to end, but it never ended soon enough for me.

For a long time I could not make sense of the nightly picture that played itself out in front of my eyes. This person, who gave birth to me and had proved she loved me in so many ways, could be seen now towering over me, gritting her teeth and refusing to stop the pain she was inflicting on me.

I did not understand then, but I do now. She could have so easily turned her back and given up on me. She could have walked away from those nightly confrontations, but she knew in her heart that wouldn't be love. Despite the personal hell she was going through, she would not quit giving her all to me, for me, so that I might have a better life. She never gave in. She was right all those times she told me "it had to be done," and somehow God gave her the strength to see it through. His Grace was sufficient for her too.

Chasing The Wind

Chapter 18

Level Ground

Summertime in south Texas requires some adjustment. Everyone says it's not the heat but the humidity that makes it bad. Getting baked in an oven or steamed in a wok will provide the same outcome, so the argument was a mute point as far as I was concerned. It was just downright hot, and the cactus and mesquite trees provided little shade.

There were only a few weeks of summer left before I would start public school. My brother, James, had received his drivers permit and was proud, that at sixteen, he was now mature enough to burn up the roads between Elkers trailer park where we lived, and the small town of Carrizo Springs, less than three miles away.

James had convinced my mother and dad to let him drive me to the Carrizo Springs public pool for an afternoon of summertime fun. That was the day I met Ann. I had no idea how she would change my life in the years to come. Through her friendship, I not only would find a church home but would be able to start school with the confidence knowing I had made several new friends. Over the next five years she would become the sister I never had, and the sister-in-law my brother hoped I would have.

While I sat on the hood of my parent's car outside the chain link fence that surrounded the public pool, I knew that swimming with all those kids was out of the question. My legs were still too weak to go without my crutches and I was embarrassed at how skinny they were. My scars were hard to hide in a swimsuit and the reaction from most people who saw them still bothered me inside.

I would one day grow out of that and learn to look at them as symbols of courage and see them as the thumb print of God's protective hand on my life. But not that day! So, I watched in long pants and thought of how cool the water must feel on a day like that. Ann Lansford was my age and knew James from the previous school year.

Everyone in Carrizo knew my brother. He was one who walked around the high school campus quietly and most had learned to leave him alone. I think he learned to fight, taking up for me when we were little. Kids can be cruel at times about things they don't understand and my brother was not one to take too much time explaining it to them. If they laughed or snickered at his little brother he was on them before they saw it coming.

I am sure that my over-confidence and lack of appreciation of my limitations combined with a mouth that always had something to say in return, caused him a lot of bumps and bruises. I know he must have loved me or it would not have hurt him so much for other kids to be cruel to me. James was rough and tumble all the way, but he had a big heart.

After James introduced us, Ann talked to me through the fence. She visited with me on and off all afternoon. She seemed to understand that I needed a friend and it was obvious she was a good girl with the love of Christ in her dimpled face and a wide friendly smile. Over and over she would jump off the high dive and then pop up by the fence to ask me what dive she could do for me next.
She was doing for me what she knew I could not do for myself. With a pool of friends around her, she still took the time to befriend

a stranger through a chain link fence. As the sun went down, I thought of how I had enjoyed my day at the pool, even though I had remained high and dry on the hood of my parent's beige Oldsmobile Ninety Eight.

I was nervous my first day at Carrizo Springs Junior High. The principal, Mr. Jackson, was kind and understanding about the years I had spent being tutored in the hospital. My transcripts were spotty at best and it was obvious that I should have been placed back to the seventh grade. I had not completed the seventh grade due to a year filled with battling infections and living in isolation.

In spite of my lack of seventh grade skills, Mr. Jackson promoted me on to the eighth grade. He looked at me the day I registered for school and said, "You seem like a smart boy; you need to stay up with the kids your own age."

Wow, I had skipped the seventh grade all together. I was excited about the fact I had jumped a full grade and could not believe my good fortune, but I had no idea how difficult that leap, of so called good fortune, would end up being.

I soon learned the extent of what I didn't know. I struggled in Math and English. It was like putting together a puzzle that not only had pieces missing but had no picture on the box for a point of reference. I had to work twice as hard to keep up with my classmates. I often felt stupid and inferior to the kids in my class.

My life experiences to this point were so different than the kids with whom I was now going to school. But there was always music. Somewhere between all the notes and key signatures, I found equal footing. God knew the things I would need to feel normal. He knew my frustration long before I would experience it; His infinite wisdom had created the solution.

I now lived in a world where all I had to do was stand up and walk around and everyone would know I was different. At Scottish Rite there was never any finger pointing or gawking. No one stood out like a sore thumb. Not only were we equal in the eyes of the staff, but in each others as well. I soon realized this haven didn't exist in the real world.

It was there and then that I decided, if I were going to be different, it was going to be for the things I chose instead of what I had no control over. Music was my gift from God and it leveled the playing field and eventually led to my acceptance. I was never part of what you would call the "in crowd" or one of the hot kids, but I had friends who were. I tried to be a friend to every segment represented in our school. The cowboys, affectionately known as "goat ropers," Hispanics, rockers, dopers and the nerds were all my friends.

I couldn't ask others not to judge me by what they saw on the outside if I turned around and judged them in the same way. I honestly did not see any of them in that way. They were just my friends and what they wore, how they looked or how they spoke did not mean a thing to me. I accepted them all and they accepted me.

It was later that their acceptance of me grew into respect and pride and that, in turn, created a strong confidence in my life. They would become proud of me and I would be proud to be called their friend.

Junior High band and choir were where I stepped onto that level playing field and where Mr. Leeth, the band and choir director would become my mentor, my teacher, and close friend. He had a passion for music and he loved teaching it to the young and hungry. I was hungry as hungry could get and I wanted to learn it all.

I started singing at the school PTA functions and news quickly spread. The local Lions Club, Rotary Club, FFA, and 4H were where I tortured my audiences as I learned how to give a performance. The hardest part was getting over stage fright. I never let the audience know, but I was always just a few seconds away from "up-chucking a lunch monkey".

It seemed I was always asked to sing at a function where there was a meal planned. If they had only known what an awful situation laid brewing just under the surface, I probably would not have been invited to sing. I tried not to eat before I sang, and now you know the real reason why. It has nothing to do with breath control or indigestion or having to wait for thirty minutes or you'll get cramps (or is that swimming? I forget), but I tried not to let my nerves show, and most people never knew.

Did you know the National Anthem is one of the most difficult songs to sing? I learned that firsthand when I began singing it at all the hometown football games. It became a tradition that filled me with pride. Many people commented over the years on how they enjoyed hearing it sung, but they never knew how it thrilled me to sing it for them. Standing in front of my hometown and hearing them sing along with me while holding their right hand over their heart sent chills down my spine every time. It was an honor to have been asked to represent them, banding together to show our patriotism for all visiting teams and fans. Of all my high school memories it stands out as one of the best.

Ann Lansford had introduced me to a lot of people who, over time, became some of my closest friends. The Baker girls, the Howard kids, the Box family, and the Jackson girls, were some of those friends just to name a few. Most of those came from my church youth group. Preston Taylor Jr. and Marsha Taylor were the preacher's kids and when I was not at their house you could find Preston at mine.

Preston Jr. was, and still is, a character that defies description. His brilliant imagination and quick wit provided us with many fun-filled days at church. We were always into something. Like the time he and I went to put up revival posters around town for his father Preston Taylor, Senior. We were glad to do it, but sadly, less than an hour into out task, we ran out of scotch tape. We searched his father's car for something we could use and found a package of double-sided tape in the glove box.

We were in luck, or so we thought. It was later on that it was brought to our attention that the fliers that were now placed in every store window in town were held in place with Mr. Taylor's toupee tape. If it was a secret that he had a hairpiece, then the rug was out of the bag now, and signs of it were all over town. I don't think Brother Taylor saw as much humor in it as we did. I could say he flipped his lid, but I won't.

The First Baptist Church of Carrizo Springs was a great church to grow up in. I sang in the adult choir as well as the youth choir. There were even times I led the music for church services. Ann Lansford and I sang a lot of specials in that church. We formed a singing group called "The Believers" and sang at many 4H functions and competitions as well as rodeo and livestock shows throughout Texas.

The kids in our singing group were so talented. We won many awards over the years. I sang the lead part but it was the harmonies they sang that made everyone take notice. The group was comprised of Marsha and Susan Tollett, Steven John, Ann Lansford, and me. We had a lifetime of experiences in just a few years, and it became such a time of growth for me that I still find it easy to recall today.

It was in this group of four friends that I started down the path of using my talents to glorify Christ. It was a path that grew narrow at times and I shamefully admit that I wandered in the wilderness for a spell, but God was patient and gentle. Step by sometimes painful step, God gently guided my feet back where His perfect plan for my life was waiting.

Mr. Leeth had his hands full as a music teacher. He was both the band and choir director, demanding a level of excellence from us and he worked hard to get it. UIL (Inter-Scholastic) competitions at the district, regional and state levels were where we needed to shine the most. It would have a direct bearing on scholarship opportunities at universities we might want to attend later.

The judges of these competitions were always college professors recruiting new talent for their respective departments. Competition was fierce and everyone wanted to come home with a #1 rating. This meant you were the best on that day for your given instrument. I competed in the percussion, vocal ensemble, and solo male vocalist categories.

Mr. Leeth was the driving force and the reason for any and all of my successes throughout high school. He polished my talent and never let me settle for an inferior performance. Because of his drive, I achieved a #1 rating in district, regional and state for four years in a row.

We all wore our medals on our letter jackets and, with my limp and uneven gait, they would bang together making a lot of noise. When I walked the halls of school it sounded like Santa's sleigh coming in for a landing. Everybody always knew when I was coming and I wore those medals with great pride.

My first #1 rating at state was as much of an accomplishment for Mr. Leeth as it was for me. He told me I was the first of his vocal students to achieve that honor. He made me wear my medal all the way home that day. We traveled to Austin in his car instead of a school bus because I was the only student to make it to state that year.

Stopping in a small town for supper that night, Mr. Leeth would not let me take off the medal before going inside. I felt uneasy about keeping it on but he said, "You worked for it and you earned it, so be proud of it." He was quick to tell everyone who asked just what it was for. It was hard to tell which one of us was proudest of our accomplishment. I could not have gotten as far as I did without the talents of a caring, giving and gifted teacher like Mr. Leeth.

My high school years flew by so fast that even now it seems like a blur. When my senior year rolled around, I saw big changes happening around me. My brother had up and joined the navy and Mr. Leeth had left for a new teaching job, and we had moved into a new high school facility. They were all signs that my life was approaching some major changes.

My cup arthroplasties were starting to fall apart and I could not hide the pain. I guess four and a half years of marching at halftime in band and in countless parades had taken its toll on my hips.

I was always competitive and an organized sport was something I wanted to participate in but I knew baseball and football, not to mention track and field, were out of the question for me. I did have an advantage in one area. I had a powerful upper body due to all my years on crutches and pulling myself around with my arms, and I found that I could peel the cover off of a golf ball.

I had no idea which way the ball was going after I hit it but I knew one thing, that it would be a long walk to recover any of my hard hit balls.

I spent two years playing golf for my high school team and I loved the game. I was always a hacker, not a striker, but it didn't matter to the team or the school. They gave me every opportunity to prove myself and never once coddled me or said I was not physically able to do something. They gave me the chance to figure out my limitations on my own. I began to cross over those limits at the end of my junior year.

I really did push my hips past their structural limits. I held nothing back and took on life at a breakneck speed. I could not take it easy. I believed, "to those who were given much, much would be required" and I had been blessed beyond measure. But, by my senior year, I was literally on my last leg. I didn't play golf that year and I'm sure that's the reason they did so well in the season. All I wanted to do was prove that I had the ability to be like everyone else.

When the annual sports banquet came around my senior year, I was awarded a plaque that named me the outstanding athlete of the year. We all knew I was not given that honor for my athletic prowess. It was the real athletes themselves who came up with the award idea in the first place. The award had nothing to do with ability and everything to do with heart.

They were showing their appreciation for my effort, my determination and my willingness to participate. I was allowed to get in the game, be a part of the action, and prove to myself that I didn't have to just stand and watch. They let me be one of them, and I gave it all I had. That night they showed me it had not gone unnoticed, and that giving it "my all" had been enough.

As I started thinking of my senior year and where I would go to college, I had to factor in the possibility of more surgeries. Would I be physically able to attend a university if accepted? I didn't know the answer but I had lived my life understanding that all things are possible for those who love the Lord.

In an answer to prayer, I received an invitation to travel to Hardin Simons University in Abilene, Texas, to audition for a vocal scholarship. I wanted also to play in the infamous, Hardin Simmons Cowboy Marching Band, but I wasn't sure if my hips were going to allow that this time.

The campus was beautiful with a top-notch music department. My aunt and uncle lived less than an hour from campus in the small town of Clyde, so I would not be without family. It would be a perfect place for me to continue my education. I liked what I saw at HSU and as I auditioned for them, I hoped they liked what they heard.

After returning from my weekend trip to Abilene, I was faced with a senior year that in some respects was not what I had hoped it would be. I missed Mr. Leeth and the thought of graduation without him didn't seem right. He was not there to celebrate with me when my letter of acceptance to Hardin Simmons along with a vocal scholarship came in the mail. The news left me feeling sad at a time that I should have been happy. I could not share it with the one person that played such a big part in why I had a scholarship in the first place. I wanted him to be proud.

One of the biggest surprises of my last year in school was to receive the National Arion Award for outstanding vocal achievement. This honor was given to a graduating senior from a nation-wide list of students. I am sure Mr. Leeth submitted my name along with my qualifications for review before leaving Carrizo a year earlier. He was also the reason I was named to Who's Who of American High School Students. He took the time to make sure I was recognized for my accomplishments in the face of my adversities.

The funny thing is that, in all of my competitions, I never worked for the awards or medals. I worked for Mr. Leeth and his approval and the medals and awards came when his standards were met. When you love someone, you strive to meet their expectations and in doing so you're lifted to heights that you could not have ascended to alone. I guess in a strange way the Arion medal signified to me that Mr. Leeth made it to my graduation after all.

I stood there in my purple cap and gown on the fifty- yard line for our commencement ceremony and sang the National Anthem, one last time, for the school I loved. I guess my classmates and the people watching this rite of passage understood that a tradition was coming to a close.

When I hit the last note, and as tears rolled down my cheeks, the senior class behind me and the crowd in the stands in front of me erupted into an explosion of spontaneous applause. It was a response of love and gratitude unlike anything I had ever experienced before.

I don't know how long they stood and clapped, it seemed like forever and for me, time stood still. The roar of voices, coming from behind me as well as in front, had me trapped between them in a thank you embrace that would never be forgotten. It was as if they wanted to savor the moment, stretch it out and make it last as long as they could for the last time, and so did I.

I was off to Hardin Simmons for my freshman year, but I was not the only one destined for Abilene.

There was one other senior from Carrizo Springs that had applied and had been accepted as well. I guess after singing together so long, she knew I was no good without her. My best friend, Ann Lansford, came along to make sure I did it right. Ann, the sister I never had, was still watching over me just like the first day at the pool so many years before.

William Boyd Chisum

Chasing The Wind

Chapter 19

No Turning Back

I saw Ann as often as we could get together that first year, but the university was large and our dorms were on opposite sides of the campus. I was still struggling physically and just getting to some of my classes became a battle.

We would get together at the cafeteria for lunch or at the Baptist student union meetings. We sang together as much as we could, but in a place that crowded, it was easy for us to drift apart.

After awhile we ran in different circles but our friendship never faded. At the end of our first semester, Ann was invited to become a foreign exchange student through the Rotary Club back in Carrizo. She would be going to Australia for a year and live with a host family outside Sydney.

I was thrilled for her but I knew my second semester would not be the same without her. I'm glad in a way that she wasn't around for the second semester. I didn't want her to see me struggle. Ann had a take control, "I can fix it," type of personality but what I was going through she could not fix. This was a dive she could not do for me.

A big fish in a small pond will stand out even if he doesn't want to, but take that big fish and put him in a large lake with countless other big fish, and he's just one of many other fish. This idea was never truer than it was my freshman year at Hardin Simmons.

I had received a vocal scholarship, but so had many others. I found out why they received theirs. It was because they were the best I had ever heard. I guess I shouldn't have been shocked having seen the talent scattered about in all my competitions, but never had I seen such a large group of God-gifted individuals at one time and in one place.

Choir rehearsals and vocal labs were like standing in heaven's choir room. I just wanted to sing softly so I could hear everyone else.

My vocal instructor had determined in his mind that I would some-day be a well-known opera tenor. He spent the first semester trying to convince me I would like it, and I spent the second semester proving to him I would not. I loved singing in choir and the vocal ensembles.

I enjoyed learning the mechanics of sound and vocal support and musical supposition, composition and the overall anatomy of music. I realized that somewhere along the way a degree in music was someone else's dream. I was just a small town Texas boy with a machine gun vibrato. My roots ran too deep and even though my professor tried, I could not be transplanted into that Pavarotti garden he had prepared for me in his mind.

I was disillusioned and frustrated with where I was headed. I did not set out to teach music -- I wanted to perform music -- and not with the London Philharmonic Orchestra, unless they knew any Dallas Holms, Andrea Crouch or Gaither music, then we could talk about it.

Southern gospel and contemporary gospel music were somewhat frowned upon by my professors as being an inferior form of musical expression. Their idea of what I should sing was just not my cup of tea, so as my first year reached its end, the music department and I reached one as well.

I left Hardin Simmons after my freshman year. I was back in Carrizo Springs trying to figure out my life and the direction I needed to go. Dad had made an appointment for me to see an orthopedic surgeon in San Antonio to evaluate what could be done to relieve the pain I was experiencing and increase my mobility.

Dr. Butler came highly recommended and because I was listed as a full time student, my dad's Blue Cross and Blue Shield insurance would cover anything that would be necessary. I wondered what technologies had developed since my cup arthroplasties were done five and a half years earlier.

Dr. Butler looked at the x-rays and commented that both cups were loose and needed to come out and that if I decided to go ahead with their removal we would only have one option to choose from. He asked if I was in more pain than I could handle, and I told him yes.

"The reason I ask," he said, "is that once we make the decision to start down this road there will be no turning back." He said he wished we could put off doing anything for another twenty years. I told him I didn't think that was possible.

He then began describing the procedure he had in mind, known as a Total Hip Replacement. He said, "What we will do is remove the metal cups that are loose, saw off the end of the femur just below the ball that is supposed to go into the socket. The femur is the long bone that runs from your hip to your knee. Once we change the anatomical structure we can't go back and undo it. After the end of the femur is removed, the middle of the femur itself is hollowed out so that a steel shaft can then be cemented into it. The sockets will be reshaped to accommodate a man-made socket that will also be cemented into place.

The downside is that it is a hard surgery on the body, and the risk is high for blood clots that can cause pulmonary embolisms or blood clots in the lungs." Then he gave me the 'really good news.' "The cement is not permanent. If we do this, the life expectancy of the procedure would be, at best, twelve years. This procedure is rarely if ever done on a nineteen year old. It was developed for senior citizens with femur fractures or severe rheumatoid arthritis."

I slowly let his words sink in. I quickly added and subtracted my life expectancy after the first surgery. I would have to have one or both hips replaced every ten to twelve years and that was based on the activity level of a senior citizen.

I realized this surgery would not be the end of the road that I was looking for. He gave no options other than a wheelchair or crutches for the rest of my life. He said, as he left, that nothing had to be decided today and that we should go home and give him a call when we were sure of what we wanted to do.

My mind was numb as I tried to understand the decision that had to be made. As we left his office for the drive home, my dad and I discussed each other's feelings about the risks and benefits of the surgeries.

A wheelchair might be the way to go my dad told me, but I knew his heart was not in his suggestion. He knew how hard I had fought to walk and to give up now, at only nineteen, was something I was not sure I could do.

It was nearly an hour into our drive when I finally came out and asked him what I should do. He thought for a moment and looked over at me and said, "I can't tell you what to do anymore. With the risks being what they are, and the certainty of a lifetime of surgeries to come, I can't make your decision for you. If I told you to do it and it turned out wrong, I couldn't live with myself. You'll have to live with your choice long after I'm dead and gone, so think it through before you decide."

I understood the helplessness in the tone of his voice and we road the rest of the way home having little conversation. "What should I do," I cried out in my brain. I was only nineteen and forced to make a decision that would affect the rest of my life. I had so many dreams and aspirations and none of them included crutches or wheelchairs.

I had two doors to choose from and either one would change the course of my life. I longed to start the morning over again when the only choices I had to make were what to wear, what music to listen to, or where to go to school. We pulled into the driveway of Elkers Trailer park and slowly went inside to explain to mom what Dr. Butler had said.

Mom was not happy with the options we were given and wanted me to wait. Dad repeated to her that this was going to have to be my choice and no one else's. All I knew was that I did not want to face life the way I had for the past year. I was not afraid of pain, I lived with it everyday. I was not really afraid of the surgery either. I was more afraid of never seeing my dreams realized than I was anything else. I could handle the risks and all the future surgeries as long as it provided me a small chance to reach my dreams the way I dreamt them, standing on two feet and walking.

Less than an hour after returning home, my decision was made. I asked Dad to call and schedule the surgery. The Lord had given me a peace as I stood in the shadow of this mountain I had to climb, but I also knew if I ever got tired of climbing, God would lift me up and carry me to the top. His grace would be sufficient.

I checked into the Community Hospital in mid-May for the first of two Total Hip Replacements. I was actually a little bit nervous about what the morning would bring. How would I feel after it was over? Would I be in much pain and for how long? As I thought of what the next few days would hold for me, I couldn't help but feel some excitement as well. I was breaking new ground and I could not wait to get this process started.

Chasing The Wind

Chapter 20

Ready For the Fight

I don't know how my parents spent those hours waiting for me to come out of surgery. I know I had the easier part to play. I would sleep through it all and time would stand still for me but Mom and Dad had to watch each agonizing minute come and go.

The first thing I was aware of was the mist from my oxygen mask floating in front of my eyes like an early morning fog. I kept hearing someone saying "You're in recovery Boyd, it's all over."

My throat was too sore to talk from the tube they had inserted to help me breathe, so I just nodded my head as if to say I understand. I heard Dr. Butler asking me if I could feel this. I could not understand what "feel this" meant. I opened up my eyes to find Dr. Butler poking me with a needle up and down my left leg. These pain drugs were really good I thought to myself, I don't feel anything. He asked me to wiggle my toes and I did, but strangely enough only the toes on my right foot were moving.

I must be dreaming, I thought and kept on trying to slip back into the peacefulness of my sleep, but Dr. Butler's emphatic voice kept me coming around to reality. "Can you feel this? Boyd, move your toes for me." Something had gone wrong, but my body was too tired to care. It would all be better once I got some rest. I really wasn't paralyzed from the knee down on my left side. I couldn't be. I just needed some rest and I'd be just fine. So I closed my eyes to escape the truth.

Once the effects of anesthesia wore off, I could no longer hide from it. My body had undergone an electrical short circuit from my left knee down to my toes brought on by a damaged sciatic nerve that at best had been stretched too far or at worse was now severed completely. My brain was sending a signal saying pick up, but my leg kept saying there's no one at home.

My first attempt at a Total Hip Replacement had gone terribly wrong. I now faced the question of what would go wrong with the other total hips I was destined to have in the future. What I thought would insure my chance at accomplishing my dreams was now the very thing that put those dreams in jeopardy.

If I was going to get past this, I would have to fight harder and have more faith than I had ever had before. After a few days of mental adjustment, I was ready for the fight.

My physical therapy consisted of strengthening exercises along with electrical stimulation of the nerves in my left leg. A plastic orthotic was made for me to hold my foot upright while I slept. It would ensure my foot would stay in a neutral position. Plantar flexion is when you point your toes to the ground like a ballerina and due to the loss of muscle control; my foot was in a constant state of plantar flexion.

Without the plastic orthotic to keep my foot in a neutral position, my Achilles tendon would shorten up making it impossible to ever walk again. I had to have a brace made for my shoes. My left leg and foot were useless to me and flopped around like a fish out of water when I tried to walk with out my brace. I literally had to look down to see if my foot was on the floor properly or not.

Dr. Butler was not sure if the feeling and muscle control would ever return. He said time would tell coupled with a lot of work. I was determined to work hard and did for many weeks without any improvement.

I would lie in bed each night and mentally try to will my toes to move. I would at times breakout in a sweat from straining so hard. That night was like many other nights. At first I thought it was my imagination. Did my big toe move a millimeter or not? I tried to get it to repeat and it wouldn't. It must have just been wishful thinking. I quit for awhile but the question kept rolling around in my mind. Did I or didn't I? I decided to try it one more time.

With the night light over my hospital bed on as brightly as it would go, I strained and concentrated again. Suddenly it was not my imagination. My big toe jerked as if it had been touched by an electric cattle prod. I screamed for someone to come into my room. I needed a witness to prove I was not going crazy.

My nurse came running in and I asked her to watch my toe. She looked at me as if I had gone mad but understood as I pointed at my foot. "Watch," I said. It moved again and we both were so excited. Thank you Lord for this blessing, I thought. It was a sign of things to come. It was all going to come back. It might take some time, but I would get it back.

The nurse left to document the event on my chart as I called home to let my parents know the good news. It was going to come back. I would not remain paralyzed for long.

I went home to recuperate for four months. I had not regained all the feeling and muscle control as of yet, but it was coming.

Chasing The Wind

When five months had passed from my first total hip surgery, I was packed and ready to return to San Antonio for hip number two. I looked at my first surgery as a test. Would I give up or fight? I fought and was prepared to do so again.

The second surgery came and went and even though it was hard on me, I had no surprises. I was able to go home and get ready for college, and this time I was headed for a new university and a new major.

Chasing The Wind

Chapter 21

A Distant Miracle

Oklahoma State University in Stillwater, Oklahoma became my next attempt at higher education. My recuperation from both total hips had gone well and I traded in the brace I wore on my left paralyzed leg for a pair of cowboy boots. I found that the boots gave me just as much support as the brace had but with a better sense of style and flare. The feeling and muscle control in my lower left leg had all but returned leaving me with only a small deficit in range of motion and tendon strength.

OSU was a much larger school than Hardin Simmons and changing majors as well as schools was just another sign that I did not know what to do with my life. I decided that I would become a doctor.

I knew a lot about medicine from a patient's point of view, but my understanding of the amount of study it would require was grossly underestimated. In the midst of my feeble attempt to become the next Doctor Brandon Carrell, I developed a whole new appreciation for what it takes to be a physician. The sacrifice of time and relationships was more than I was prepared to give.

At that time in my life, the pursuit of a relationship became a driving force and once again academics would have to take a back seat.

Through a local church in Stillwater Oklahoma I met a young lady. We dated for several months and in the end, we made commitments to each other.

Out of respect for her privacy and caution for the feelings of those who are innocent, I will not give names or go into anymore detail concerning this relationship in the writing of this book. It was a difficult time for both of us.

When we are young we do the best with what we know, and when we know more we do better. What we would eventually learn with age however, could not come in time to save us from ourselves. In the midst of our youth we made foolish choices.

There are many things I learned from this chapter in my life but one of the most important is that God can create something miraculous out of the wreckage we leave in our rear view mirror. Even though I can only see that miracle from a distance, I am filled with love and pride all the same.

William Boyd Chisum

Chasing The Wind

Chapter 22

Chasing the Wind

I left Oklahoma and my home state of Texas for the Sandia Mountains of Albuquerque, New Mexico. I had an opportunity to start a country and western band and pursue my passion again. The dream of becoming a star had begun to pulse through my veins like an adrenaline junkie. The bright lights of fame were calling out to me and I answered its call. I started out in small places, dives really. Places that made you feel as dirty and lost as the people who came in to hear you. I finally got a break after a year.

The band and I were hired to play for Bill Smith's Caravan East. This was a franchise of well known clubs that stretched from California, Texas, and New Mexico. If you were big in Country Music and had songs in the charts, you were going to be playing one or more at Bill Smith's clubs.

As a Caravan East house band, I would have ample opportunities to become an opening act for many if not all the artists who came through the club. I was quickly becoming well known to everyone but myself. I no longer felt close to the God who held my very breath in His hands. I had moved so far out of His will that I no longer listened to His whispers calling for me to come home. I was wandering in the wilderness, worshiping the idol I saw in my bathroom mirror each and every morning. "As a pig that returned to its wallow nightly," I would step on stage somewhere to glorify myself.

The bright lights only illuminate the star you think you want to be but it's in the surrounding shadows of the dark that you eventually see who you really are and what you've become. The darker the night, the longer it takes your eyes to adjust and see clearly. It would take me longer than most.

The band and I were not under an exclusive contract with the Caravan East so we were able to travel and do other shows as well. We had been asked to perform at the New Mexico State Fair, and while we were there I met a man who would play an important part in my future trip to Nashville. But this man, known as Otis Echols, had another place in mind for me to go to first. If I had known what awaited us, I would have never agreed to do the show.

It was a special concert for extremely unique and special people, or so I was told. I just didn't know how special and unique they really were. It could end up being best described as a free for all, full of red and blue flashing lights, loud megaphone conversations and several German Shepards and Rottweilers who effectively ran around getting to know everybody. But I'm getting ahead of myself.

Otis asked the band and me to do a concert after we finished our regular show at the New Mexico State Fair. We were told to wait until the fair was about to close its gates and then set up our equipment for an after hours show. This was to be an end of the year party for the cast and crew of the midway along with the entire carnival organization and management. It was the last night of the New Mexico State Fair and the last night of the fair season for the carnival workers as well.

We did as we were instructed and, when the lights went out on the midway for the last time that year, our stage lights went on. As we started playing, more and more of the carnival employees filtered in until we were looking at over three hundred very strange but somewhat happy people gathered around our five foot high stage. With a propensity for violence along with a large supply of free alcohol, they weren't going to remain happy for long.

We were playing one song after the other without much talking to the crowd when, all of a sudden, two girls were picked up and put on each end of the stage. I tried to ignore their antics and their feeble attempts at dancing, but dancing wasn't their only intention that night. As the clothes came off, there was no doubt in my mind that this night was going to end badly.

After the "not so wonderful" dancing instruction and the uninhibited lessons on how to stay cool, we were then asked to stop playing just long enough for them to have a drawing. It seemed that the carnival employees had been donating money all year for this one night. As they brought out the barrel covered by chicken wire with a little door on top from which the winning ticket would be drawn, the expectation and excitement level of who would get it all began to run high. But a little voice in my head was telling me something very wrong was about to happen.

Everyone got real quite as the barrel began to spin around and around. Right there on the table, in front of all to see was the object of their desire. It was a see-through Plexiglas box that held all their donated money for the year. My guess was it amounted to several thousand dollars. It was probably more money than anyone of these people had made all year. Some lucky individual was going to walk out of there that night a lot wealthier than they walked in.

Just as the barrel stopped spinning and a second before the winning ticket could be drawn, all the lights went out. They only stayed off for forty to forty five seconds, but it was still long enough. Through the darkness came a rumbling of anger along with an overwhelming feeling of betrayal. Could it be the con-artist had just been conned? When the lights came on and they saw that their money was gone, our night got real exciting, real fast.

If you've ever seen an old western barroom brawl where chairs and tables were being crushed by human bodies, this wasn't anything like that. It was a thousand times worse. When you have over three hundred drunk and very angry carnies throwing everything at each other, including each other, you find it hard to know which way to duck. I began to wonder if the barrel made from chicken wire was large enough to crawl into, but a quick glance told me it wasn't. All I knew for sure was that we had tens of thousands of dollars worth of equipment on that stage and our job was to protect it and each other if we could.

The fight went on and on for more than thirty minutes, and it showed no signs of letting up. Just when we thought it was dying down someone would wake up from their unconsciousness and get back in the game.

The guys in the band and I were holding our own using our microphone stands to keep people off the stage and away from our gear. Out of nowhere, and to our relief, we heard that help had arrived. The voice of an Albuquerque police officer on a loud speaker said they were coming in. We soon realized his words would leave us with no relief.

They were giving us five minutes to leave the premises and then they were turning the dogs loose.

Now, it took us several hours to set up our equipment and the threat of an angry dog, no matter how big he might be, was going to make tear-down happen in five minutes. What could we do? There was no way I was leaving my equipment unprotected amongst what had already been proven to me to be Ali Baba and his den of thieves. We were staying here no matter what.

As the five minutes elapsed, the fighting mass of people was still going at it. They were quickly joined by the Albuquerque canine crew, and those dogs were defiantly getting a pound of flesh for their effort.

As I watched the dogs tear into the crowd, I quickly realized those dogs didn't know the good guys from the bad guys. A quick glance around and I realized the only place we had left to go was up. On each end of the stage we had our main stacks of PA speakers and they were about ten feet tall at the top. We headed up as we watched the dogs enjoy their "buffet con-carne" and waited for the mounted police to arrive and tell us we could come down.

We never got paid for that night and I don't know if they ever found out who stole the money. Otis would owe me big for this experience but, if he could do what he said he could for me in Nashville, I'd consider the debt paid in full.

The degradation I saw that night with the carni's was just a small glimpse of what the next ten years would hold for me. God was sending me a vision, a revelation if you will of where I was headed, but it would have to get a lot worse for me to ever see it.

Chasing The Wind

Chapter 23

Nashville or Bust

Otis Echoles was a political lobbyist for the State Legislature of New Mexico. He had contacts in high places and more than just a passing fascination with the bright lights of the country music field. His father, "Pop" Echoles, was the man who wrote the country classic Sugar Time, and Otis still maintained a few Nashville contacts from those glory days. Otis also had in mind putting in place a group of investors. These investors would provide the financing needed to produce a competitive album which would, in turn, give us a better chance at a record label.

It took a little less than six months for a group of five investors to "plop down" one hundred and twenty thousand dollars for the project. Life became very hectic and I often left the front door open so my rear- end could catch up with me at the end of the day.

I was still working for the Caravan East at night but in the light of day I was working on choosing songs from producers and photo layouts, along with putting together press packets. It was all going fast and furious and surprisingly well until I started to hear the noise.

The noise sounded like plastic bubble-wrap being squeezed until it popped. At first I only heard it when I was very tired but maybe it had been there a long time and I just been too busy to notice it before. The medical term is called "crepitation." It is a grating sound heard at the ends of broken bones.

I knew I had been hurting more over the last nine months but I tried to ignore it and just attributed it to the fast life I was now living. The cemented components from my last total hip had broken apart and now the only thing holding them in place was scar tissue. As the noise in my right hip increased, my ability to move around decreased and I knew I was not going to Nashville anytime soon.

How do you break the news to a group of investors that the product they had bet on was now folding his cards before a single hand could be played? With my track record from the last two total hips I was afraid to promise anything in the way of an outcome. In this high stakes game of musical monopoly they had bought "Park Place" and I landed on the one square that would send me "straight to surgery and do not pass Music Row."

Dr. Gray was as arrogant a surgeon as I had ever met. Even his staff was afraid of his sometimes explosive behavior and his prevalent "better than everyone else" attitude. He had a God complex and, if you were his patient, you were his next creation. I had been around a lot of talented surgeons in my life and Dr. Gray would have to struggle to carry their stethoscope. Why I chose him I will never know.

Maybe it was because he could do the total hip replacement in the time frame I was looking for. But for whatever the reason I just prayed he was could repair my right hip and get me on my way.

Would the investors be there when it was all over? I didn't know and only time would tell. Once again, I had to stop my world from its rotation and get off for a while, not knowing if I would ever be allowed to get back on. I had already been through two total hips so a third would be a piece of cake.

William Boyd Chisum

I was only in the hospital for seven days. I walked out of that hospital in Albuquerque on crutches and never went back. The financial arms of my career were waiting right where I had left them and in the end we only needed to postpone the album project for three months.

I was going to Nashville, Music City USA, and I was going to turn it on its ear. Boy, was I wrong! I learned that Nashville may tremble at the site of talent but it won't fall down for it.

For every one success on music row, there's a thousand who are waiting tables or washing dishes hoping to be discovered. Some of the "has beens" or "almost was" still sing their original songs in the alleys around the Fourth Street Mission in downtown Nashville. Alcohol in one hand and evaporated dreams in the other, they still think they have what it takes.

Would that be where my dreams would end up? What made me any different from them? I had placed all my chips on the table and I was either going to win or go home. The next few years taught me that even though you win, sometimes you lose.

The recording of the album went well, and really it would have been hard for it not to when you consider the quality of the people working on it. Gene Rice was our audio engineer. He engineered Alabama's first three triple platinum albums. Joe Bob Barnhill was the producer and he also produced Roy Clark. "Pig" Robbins played keyboard along with the "A" team of Nashville's best pickers. It was the best that someone else's money could buy.

Two trips later, and the album was finally finished and ready for our first single to be released. I ended up with very little input into the selection of the single to be released. "Till Dawn Do Us Part" was the consensus of all of those who had the decision making power.

Joe Bob Barnhill had introduced my manager and the group of investors to the head of F&L Records in Nashville, and before the first pressing of "Till Dawn Do Us Part" had stopped spinning, I had signed my first recording contract.

I was ecstatic as I thought how I had convinced God to be on the same page with me concerning my life. I never gave it a thought that I was just stumbling around, nearsighted and blind, forgetting that I had already been cleansed from my sins.

I started to believe the lie, the one where I was worthy and I was good and everything that was happening to me was because I deserved it. It was the same lie that echoed down the foot paths of the Garden of Eden. Satan had opened a satellite office in Nashville and was giving away unlimited supplies of lust of the flesh, lust of the eyes and pride of life and there was a never ending line of entertainers waiting to get in line and sign up.

Satan knows that, if he gets control of those who have an influence over their adoring clamoring fans, he won't have to work so hard. The entertainers then knowingly or unknowingly become subcontractors working off Satan's blueprint for the world.

Every sin that man has ever committed or will commit can be traced to the roots of lust of the flesh, lust of the eyes and pride of life. Satan has influenced and deceived every generation since the fall of Adam in this same way. I was blinded by my own reflection and couldn't see the deception or the deceiver.

"Till Dawn Do Us Part" was released and hit the national charts at #80 with a bullet. It climbed steadily for 9 weeks ending up just out of the top 40. It did, however, make it to #6 on the "Hit Parade" out of New York. I was on my way. I went from crutches and pain and total hip number three to buses, planes and long limousines. I was living my dream.

It was all bright lights and glory for awhile until I started to see glimpses of the ugliness lurking in the shadows. I overlooked all those things and said to myself, "It'll never happen to me, I can handle this life." I saw a bass player in my band waste his life away as well as his career by being strung out on drugs from sunup to sundown. I saw country stars that I looked up to turn into womanizing drunks clothed in egotism and bitterness that would eventually drive them headfast into an early grave.

It was a lifestyle of "live fast, love hard, and die young." If the public could only have seen what went on behind the lights, behind the public relations, they would have learned that none of us were worthy of praise.

I did two tours with Keith Whitley and opened concerts for everyone you could think of from Ronnie Millsap, Alabama, Joe Stamply, Asleep at The Wheel, Sawyer Brown, and Diamond Rio. These were just a few of the artists that crossed my path over the ten-plus years that I chose to sing for the world, instead of the One who created it.

Drugs like cocaine and speed were as freely available to us as a can of coke from a vending machine. Even though I repeatedly insisted that none of "my guys" did that sort of thing, its pervasiveness would eventually ooze through the cracks, and change us all.

When a concert is over and the artist can't sleep because they're so "keyed up" from the crowd, they end up taking something to help them sleep. When they wake up groggy but still have to put on a "star image" for interviews, sound checks and all the endless things that have to be done before the next show, they end up taking something to help put the smile back on their face.

So many entertainers in this business started down that slippery slope to addiction just this way. It all too quickly becomes a vicious cycle and one that very few, once they become trapped, can ever escape.

This part of the music industry is one that nobody wants to talk about and does not limit itself to secular fields. It is the reality of fame and fortune for so many of those with whom I toured.

Sin has a dual price that will be paid; you will pay as you go and you'll pay when you arrive. You pay as you go through all the compromises you allow yourself to make, and you pay when you arrive by realizing how many people you've hurt and how much of yourself was lost in the process.

When you arrive at the destination of fame, the cashier is waiting, and the price required to get off the "not so merry-go-round" often leaves you surrounded by broken lives, addictions, and empty pockets.

There is a high price to pay mentally, physically and spiritually for the "glitter" that adorns this lifestyle as well. "Everything that coruscates with effulgence is not ipso facto aureus." It's the glitter of fool's gold that illuminates us on stage and gives us a false sense of self esteem in the eyes of those who are all too willing to pay the price of perpetual, misguided adoration. Its glow blinds them to the realization that we're just flesh and blood, and too often make mistakes, forget the words or play out of tune.

There is a national standard for tuning any musical instrument. It is known as A-440. That stands for (A) above middle (C) and, if it is in tune, it will vibrate at 440 cycles per second. This is a given rule in music. God has a standard for the harmonious tuning of our life as well and it's revealed to us by the Holy Spirit as it vibrates through the written word of God.

As a believer, you are either in tune with God's standard for your life or you're not. In other words, you're either in fellowship with God or you're not. One vibration on either side of God's 440 and you've missed the pure tone of His will for your life. For years I was able to perform with all my musical talents at 440, but my spiritual life, the thing that counted the most when all the songs had been sung, was completely and utterly out of tune.

Many people, including myself, thought that I was a 'big thing,' but I was never really a star. There's only been one star to ever walk this earth and God, in all His wisdom, used a star in the sky to illuminate where He could be found. And wise men still seek that star today.

Chasing The Wind

Chapter 24

Land Where "Enchantment" Lives

The band and I had been asked to play in Las Cruces for the New Mexico Bureau of Land Management. It was an outdoor concert at the base of the beautiful Organ Mountains. It was a special day for the State of New Mexico and the City of Las Cruces because the Organ Mountains were being turned over to the Bureau from private ownership.

The concert stage was set up under those massive peaks overlooking an open field. There were hay bales that had been brought in for people to sit on, scattered as far as the eye could see. It was an all-day concert with many local acts. We were asked to open for Michael Martin Murphy for the evening segment of the show. Standing on that stage, overlooking the thousands in the crowd, I could not help but feel insignificant in the shadows of those peaks.

God's majesty and grandeur far outweighed anything that Michael Martin Murphy or I could have produced through our feeble attempt at creativity that night. If you took the time to look up at the beauty that surrounded us, it was easy to see who the real artist was that night. It was a great concert and it gave us the opportunity to play more often in this wonderful state called The Land of Enchantment.

After the concert in Las Cruces, we were asked to play more and more in this part of New Mexico. I decided on my way back to Albuquerque that I would try to find one or two places for us to play along the way. This would break up the long trip to Las Cruses and make it more financially feasible for us to travel that far.

I found a location in Deming called the Hat Creek and another in Silver City known as the Drifter. I did not know that the owner of the Hat Creek would one day become the best man at my wedding, nor could I have foreseen at that time that the general manager of the largest radio station in this part of New Mexico would be my wife.

All those changes were going to come about in the next eighteen months. Some of those changes would put an end to my career in country music. I would be faced with a choice and when the time came it would be the easiest choice I would ever make.

We were about an hour into the show when I saw her walk in. She made her way to a table in the back of the room and sat down. I thought to myself how beautiful she was and that I would try to find out who she was when we went on break. I was not sure she had even noticed me and my uncertainty was confirmed when I looked back again and found that she had already left. She'd walked out before I could learn her name or could make sure she knew mine. It wasn't until my next trip to Silver City that we would meet face to face in a situation she could not so easily run away from.

We were back in Silver City and my first single with F&L records was still being played on regular rotation at the local radio station. By this time the recording had peaked and started that all too fast "death roll" that all songs eventually make.

KNFT was a hundred thousand watt radio station in Silver City. "Till Dawn Do Us Part" had become a popular song in this area so the radio station asked if the guys in the band and I would come and spend an hour or two live on the air, taking phone calls and essentially becoming 'DJ's for a day.'

It all sounded like it would be a lot of fun. Usually radio interviews were boring and most disc jockeys asked the same questions. "What got you started in music? Who is your favorite artist? Who do you think you sound like?" Fluff interviews with no substance and no originality, but this seemed like it would be fun and more importantly different. I had no idea how unique and different this day would be or how running into a certain redhead would change my life for the better.

Kelly King was the on-air talent that morning followed by Ken Murphy in the afternoon. We went in and met Kelly during a commercial break. She showed the room full of records for us to choose from. We were going to play DJ for a day and we were going to be able to play the songs from artists we liked. This seemed like a crazy idea and all of us were excited as we entered the record room.

I could not believe my eyes, but there she was, right in front of me! The same girl I had seen at the Drifter weeks before. I did not get to speak with her then but I stood face to face with her now, and it was obvious she was as nervous as I was. She was as professional as she could be, but I knew what she knew. The eyes never lie when it comes to mutual attraction, and our eyes were talking and telling the truth at around a mile a minute.

Her name was Nena Marshall and she was the general manager of KNFT radio. She was absolutely the most beautiful girl I had ever seen. Nena was tall and slender and she carried herself with style and dignity. She had the kind of poise and confidence that would light up a room the minute she walked in.

I had to know more about her and so I spent the rest of the day at the radio station trying to catch glimpses of her and asking questions from anyone who would talk. Getting employees to discuss their boss was not easy, but I made it obvious to them that I was interested. I did not let her know that fact, however, for several weeks to come.

We became best friends long before I ever let her see how I was falling for her. I shared with her my life, complete with all its twists and turns. She knew my heart inside and out, long before she took up residence there.

Jack Moulton was Nena's stepfather and he wanted to be the "Boss Hog" of this "would be Dukes of Hazard" town known as Silver City. He was also the owner of KNFT Radio. Jack had his hand in almost everything that happened in Silver City, good and bad, directly or indirectly from financial to political. He was an influential entity to be dealt with.

Jack ran in big circles and was even friends with the two New Mexico United States Senators. He even had a hand in getting his own personal attorney appointed District Judge. He had friends in high places and in places I did not care to know about.

Jack's best friend and associate in many business and non-business escapades was a man named Jim Decker. Decker was chairman of the board of the largest bank in Silver City. He was also the person who suggested that Jack should be as controversial as possible as a strategy to increase revenue for the radio station. The idea worked well, but even Decker could not have imagined the extent to which Jack would take it.

Together Silver City became their playground. It was as if they were connected at the hip, and wherever you saw one you saw the other. They made many profitable, as well as some not so profitable deals and had many more exploits than can be exposed in this book.

It is a powerful tool to have a hundred thousand watt radio station as your own personal megaphone, and Jack never hesitated to use it. I said all that to say this, if Jack didn't like you, he had the ability to make your life miserable. This was a fact that I was soon to learn.

Of all the things Jack loved in his life, his stepdaughter Nena ranked somewhere at the top of his list. Jack had a reputation of protecting the things he had a vested interest in. In his mind, no one was going to be good enough for Nena, especially a country music singer who he saw as a gypsy bum.

Jack had more of a doctor or a successful lawyer in mind for Nena and, even then, they might not pass his IQ test. I was the last thing on his list of suitable son-in-laws but, fortunately for me, Nena had her own criteria.

Jack was not around when Nena and I first met and started dating. But just like a bad habit, he showed up soon enough. In my eyes, Nena was perfect and really only had one major flaw and that was Jack. Fortunately for me, Nena had no intentions of following Jack's mental blueprint for her life and that fact alone set the stage for many confrontations.

Months passed and Nena and I had been dating for almost a year. She put thousands of miles on her Nissan 300ZX traveling around New Mexico and parts of Texas to follow my concerts and shows. The members in the band were noticing more and more that I was losing interest in the direction our music was taking us. I had always told myself that when I found someone I loved more than what I was doing, I would quit. I am sure they knew that Nena was the real thing and that our time together as a band was coming to an end.

I had experienced all the admiration and "star" like lifestyle I could stomach with all the sordid benefits one could imagine. In the end it only left me feeling empty and ashamed. I had hurt so many people in my country music pursuits and along the way I left a long list of regrets behind me. I had become a man I didn't recognize. It was as if all I was doing was chasing the wind and in the end I realized it was all in vain.

My eyes were fixed on a worldly dream. I was not only in that world, but I had become that world. It is impossible to wallow in the mud and not get it all over you. Fortunately for me, Nena could see past all the glitter of my persona and the bright lights of this lifestyle to the person I had buried inside so many years ago.

I had been everything to everyone for so long that I lost who I really was. To say I had developed an ego would be the biggest understatement in the world. It becomes so easy to believe your own press releases and once you start doing that, reality flies out the window along with your humility. But, in the quiet darkness of the night when I found myself alone with God, the Holy Spirit never failed to convict me of my countless actions and over time it broke down the walls I had built to keep the truth out.

I was a living, breathing Dorian Gray painting, and the ugliness of my life was exposed for God and me to see. I needed to come back home where my Holy Father was waiting for me with open arms. I was a twentieth century version of the prodigal son who was now pulling himself out of the pigsty and starting that long walk home. I did not know what lay ahead for me, but I knew anything was better than the way I was living my life now.

I could never be the kind of husband or father God wanted me to be until I first went back and picked up the pieces of the man God intended me to be. These were pieces that sin, like a chisel, had sheared off my Christian life, leaving me out of God's perfect will and under His chastening hand.

While I watched my country music career crumble around me, I thought of all the time I had wasted achieving a worthless goal. At one time or another, I had singles playing in nearly every radio station in the country. I had stood on the Grand Old Opry and toured with some of the biggest names in country music.

It might be hard to understand how a person could be glad to see this come to an end, but I was. I had grown to hate singing about all those "Achy Breaky Hearts" and "Blue Eyes Crying in the Rain." Those sordid songs and the lifestyle that came with them were destroying my life, leading me further away from the person God had intended me to be. I think it was a combination of me walking away from that life style and God the Father finally having seen enough of the wreck I had made of his permissive will, which brought me to my knees begging forgiveness for the Christian life I had squandered. God, once again in love, reached out his hand and tuned the strings of my life.

Chasing The Wind

Chapter 25

"Two Shall Be As One"

Nena Marshall had agreed to become Nena Chisum and I was walking on cloud nine. But in the midst of our excitement, Nena was going through a hard time knowing she would soon lose a grandmother she loved dearly. Her grandmother had been ill for sometime and Nena was at her hospital bedside every free moment she could find. It was in those final days of a loved one that I first met Nena's mom Kaylla.

Kaylla and Jack resided in Scottsdale, Arizona. I think all she knew about me she had either learned from conversations with Nena on the phone or gleaned from Jack's infrequent visits to Silver City to check on his radio station. I was not quite sure which version of me she believed. That made me feel uneasy as Nena and I entered the hospital to meet Kaylla at the bedside of her terminally ill mother. Nena had told me so much about her family but, even though I felt like I already knew them, I wondered if I was intruding on a family of which I was not yet a part.

As we stepped off the elevator, Nena saw her mom standing in the hall waiting for us. I was so nervous not knowing what she might already think of me, that I struggled to find words to say. Kaylla came over and gave me a hug and, from somewhere in my apprehensiveness, I blurted out the words, "Kaylla, if Nena looks like you when she is your age, we will definitely be getting married."

Kaylla was beautiful and, even in those tense moments in dealing with the impending loss of her mother, she had an air of class and dignity about her. We all had a big laugh at my forwardness and I guess it broke the ice. I believe it also set the tone for a close relationship with her that developed over the next few years. She was destined to become, not just my mother-in-law but, an adopted second mother through marriage who I would love dearly.

We all went into Nena's grandmother's room. Waiting just inside the door was Nena's Aunt Madelyn, Kaylla's sister, who was keeping watch over their mother, who was in the last days of her life. As I listened to all of them tell stories of how wonderful this woman was, I could not help but feel a sense of loss in not having the opportunity to know her. She was in the deepest, darkest shades of life on earth and was about to step into the light of eternal glory. She did not know we were there and, even if she did, I don't think she cared. She was not listening to earthly voices anymore.

The family asked me to sing at the funeral service and I was honored to do so. It was the first time I had the chance to meet all of the extended family of sisters, nieces, nephews, aunts and uncles. With all the family in for the service, the tension brewing underneath the surface between Jack and me was put aside. We didn't talk and Jack found it hard to even look in my direction most of the time. However, the tension would soon resurface. After everyone went home from the funeral, it increased to a point of volcanic proportions. Even I could not believe the extent to which Jack would go to keep this marriage between Nena and me from taking place.

With my country music career gone, Nena had hired me to work at the radio station. This was like gasoline on an already raging fire for Jack. He was not consulted in the hiring, just as he was not consulted in Nena's decision to marry me. For a man whose picture could be found in the dictionary above the words "control freak," his lack of control in this situation just drove his resentment of me to a fevered pitch.

To Jack I was just a nuisance. I was literally just a speed bump on his autobahn of life. He was sure I would fade away as fast as I had appeared. When he realized I was not going anywhere, he figured I might need a little help with the directions out of town.

It had only been a few weeks since the funeral of Nena's grandmother when Jack drove into the radio station parking lot that day. When I saw him, I knew we were about to go face-to-face and toe-to-toe, and I was determined to win. In fact I had already won; he just couldn't accept it. He was determined to try one more time to break us up. He had finally come to the realization that he could not only be losing a daughter but he also saw the possibility of losing his radio station manager. With Jack now spending so much time in Scottsdale, Nena had become the real reason and driving force behind KNFT radio station's success. I was not only rearranging his personal life but our marriage could possibly have a major effect on his financial life as well. I was a threat to his heart as well as his wallet.

As he stormed in the radio station and walked past my office where I was busy pretending to write advertising copy, he cut me a glance and with a stern voice said "you and I are going to lunch so get ready." I suddenly lost any appetite I might have had but, we weren't going to eat anyway so it didn't matter.

I quickly wrapped up my work and waited outside by his white Cadillac. The heat emanating off the hood bore a striking resemblance to Jack's forehead as he walked into the station. He had driven in from Scottsdale and the drive had given him plenty of time to work up a good head of steam.

Jack was taking me to the Red Barn restaurant for our "power lunch" but Jack didn't realize when it came to this situation he was powerless. The Red Barn was always Jack's place of choice when he was going to meet with someone who he wanted to dominate and intimidate. It gave him a sense of control to meet there because the mayor of Silver City owned it. This was the same mayor Jack was instrumental in getting elected. Jack liked being surrounded by those things he had either accomplished or conquered, and I was determined to be neither.

The waitress brought us our order and we pretended to be hungry as both of us waited to see who would light the fuse first. I started the conversation by telling him how much I loved Nena and tried to convince him that we knew what we were doing. He expressed, in no uncertain terms, that he not only thought I was dumber than dirt, but was sure that Nena had completely lost her mind.

Finally, Jack reached into his coat and pulled out his checkbook. Just when I thought our battle of wills was over and that he going to write a check to pay for lunch, the final insulting blow came.

Jack looked me straight in the eye and asked how much money it was going to cost him to get me out of Silver City by the end of the day. I shot back that there was not enough money in the bank for that to ever happen. He angrily responded that I had no idea how much money he had in his bank account. Through gritted teeth he asked again, "How much money is it going to take?" As he pointed his pen at me, Jack said, "Everybody has a price, what's yours?"

My love for Nena was not for sale. I told him no amount of money was going to change my mind. We were getting married and he could spend his money on the materials he needed to build a bridge, and get over it.

As we drove back to the radio station, the tension so thick you could've cut it with a knife. I just couldn't trust Jack with anything sharp at that time.

With the wedding date set, Nena and I made plans for our future together. My parents were not able to come to New Mexico for the wedding. As we made our plans, we were not at all sure how many people would show up from Nena's side of the family either.

We had planned a simple ceremony at the courthouse to be followed by a reception at the radio station. We had no help from anyone with the planning or decorations with the exception of a few of the radio station personnel. There was no rehearsal dinner or ceremony walk through. We couldn't afford either. Kaylla may have wanted to help but I am sure Jack made that very difficult for her. No, we were forced to do it all on our own, with considerable resistance from some of the people who should have been making this the most beautiful day in Nena's life.

I was the reason we had to struggle to put our wedding together. If Nena had married someone Jack thought was suitable for her, I am sure she would have had one of the biggest, grandest weddings Silver City had ever seen. But, instead, there we were planning to say "I do" in a Judge's chamber. I knew this could not have been the wedding Nena had dreamed about since she was a little girl. The cold hard realities of the situation, and Jack's resentment and unfounded preconceived ideas, had destroyed her dream of a fairy tale wedding and there was nothing I could do to get it back for her. She never once complained to me but, deep down, I knew she was disappointed. She deserved so much more than she received, from all of us.

In the end, it did not matter if anyone came for the ceremony or not. The only thing that really mattered was that she and I were there together. Hand-in-hand we would say our vows and pray that, when the judge asked if anyone present knew of any reason we shouldn't be married, for once Jack would stay seated and 'forever hold his peace.'

All those in the wedding party were scheduled to meet at the radio station one hour before the service was to begin. As Nena and I waited outside KNFT radio, we saw Nena's mother drive into the parking lot. She was driving in from Scottsdale and, as we watched her car come to a stop, it appeared at first that she made the drive alone. We were soon to realize that crouched down in the passenger seat hiding like a "Jackie in the box" was Nena's older sister Carree. It was a nice surprise for Nena and one we had not expected. We were in desperate need of wedding guests who were excited about being there.

After arriving at the courthouse, Judge Scholl didn't keep us waiting for long. He had a big smile that made you feel like you had known him all your life. He was a little man who walked with a pronounced limp, which made me feel right at home.

For days prior to standing before the judge, I had teased Nena about the fact she would have to vow to "love, honor and obey." I always put a heavy emphasis on the word obey and it had become an on- going joke between us. She said she would promise everything else, but obey was out of the question. Fortunately, the word "obey" wasn't included in our vows. However, the word "plight" did. I was so concerned about not messing up when asked to repeat my vows that, when the word "plight" came out of the judge's mouth I was dumbfounded. I guess Nena was too, because she shot me a look as if to say, "Is that another word for obey?" Neither of us knew what it meant, but we still said "I do."

I spent a good part of our honeymoon trying to convince Nena that the word plight really did mean obey. She soon found a dictionary, and that ended that.

We all went back to the radio station for our reception. The cake that we bought along with the punch was waiting for us in Jack's office. The irony of our victory lap being run in Jack's very own office was not lost on anyone, especially Jack. We hoped that he would somehow see himself clear to "bury the hatchet" and hopefully not in the back of my head.

Jack "graciously" gave us a weekend off from the radio station so we could enjoy our honeymoon. I had rented an "A" frame cabin in the mountains where we could get away and recuperate from the stress of our wedding.

It began to snow shortly after we arrived. As we snuggled by the rock fireplace in our cabin, we watched the snow flakes float slowly to the ground. It was as if a huge feather pillow in the sky had somehow torn apart and was being vigorously shaken out on the mountainside.

The snow was fresh and pure and signified a new beginning for our lives together. As we walked hand in hand through the snow we knew that we were exactly where God wanted us to be. Through all my searching, I had finally found her and somewhere deep in her heart she always knew I would come. My search was finally over and her waiting had reached its end.

William Boyd Chisum

Chasing The Wind

Chapter 26

A Thanksgiving to Remember

I told you earlier how Decker had suggested to Jack that if he would create controversy, it would garner more listeners, which would generate more advertising dollars. I promise you, Decker had no idea what he was unleashing when he encouraged Jack to become controversial. It was like inviting termites to eat wood.

He didn't become controversial just to increase revenue. He did it because he loved stirring people up and if he could stir up Democrats, he loved it even more. He always had some kind of ruckus going that would irritate them.

He hired a girl and changed her radio name to "Jill" and they did the "Jack and Jill" show from 6 to 9 a.m. He played the role of the overbearing conservative (which was not hard for him) and she played the role of the not too smart, bleeding heart liberal (which was very hard for her because she was very intelligent and was from one of the few conservative families in town).

He did a three minute editorial five days a week and it would repeat five times a day on the station. If he ran out of some local liberal issue to attack, he would fall back on Planned Parenthood, The National Education Association, Free School Breakfast and Lunch Programs, and Free Butter and Cheese give-a-ways.

Jack referred to all Democrats as "a-bunch-of-bleeding-heart-liberals." That was his standard phrase. If he just completely ran out of liberal issues to attack, he would resort to belittling the Post Office for being so slow.

He ended each editorial with, "That's my opinion, let's hear yours." It was as if he was daring them to respond.

The Board of Regents at the Western New Mexico University in Silver City had hired what Jack called a "fifty year old hippie," to be the president. He had gray hair down to his shoulders and wore jeans torn at the knees.

It was at that time that a country singing duo called "The Bellamy Brothers" had come out with a song called "Old Hippie." Each day for five days, Jack ran an editorial, taking the new president to task on some liberal issue. Jack would then play "Old Hippie" and dedicate it to the president by name.

The university president demanded equal air time, which was exactly what Jack wanted – more controversy. Jack welcomed him to the station. The president was very nervous and repeatedly bungled his responses. Four days later, he left town. Jack was floating on a cloud. He sincerely believed he had the power to run someone out of town.

Jack received a letter from one of the better known hippies in the area who called him a "rabid, radical, right-wing, renegade, ridiculous, religious republican." Jack read the letter on the air and said, "I wonder how he knew that?"

Jack was a small-town, Don Imus, with a mysterious mix of Shawn Hannity, Rush Limbaugh and a dash of Jerry Springer thrown in for the fun of it. It was a high-octane, extremely volatile mixture.

Those of us who worked at KNFT were forced into the position of having to answer for Jack's antics. As we related to him what we had to go through with listeners, he would just laugh and say, "It looks like our customers like it; they're all buying more advertising and our ratings are up."

Each Labor Day the Chamber-of-Commerce conducted a 'Strong Man Competition' among some of the extremely large, muscular men who worked at the Phelps Dodge Copper Mine, just outside of Silver City. It was basically an ore loading contest. It was always held at the park in the center of town.

One of Jack's stunts, that doubly irritated the so called 'bleeding-heart-liberals,' was a Dwarf Throwing Contest. Jack persuaded four of the 'Strong Man' competitors to participate in his "First Annual KNFT Dwarf Throwing Contest." The 'throwing' competition would be held at the City of Rocks, a State Park about 30 miles south of town, immediately following the Strong Man Competition.

Jack had carefully hand-picked the judges. During the event all the participants, judges, onlookers, and dwarfs were 'interviewed.' The whole show was 'scripted' but the audience didn't know it and it came across as a real event. The-bleeding-heart-liberals were furious.

It was not unusual for Jack to get threats on his life or have anonymous, menacing callers threaten to burn down the radio station. Jack would just laugh it off and say, "That'll be great; we'll get to remodel the place with the insurance money."

These Jack-staged events were standard operating procedure for KNFT. Jack had some kind of bazaar caper going all the time. When

Nena and I returned from our honeymoon, we knew we would be back in the middle of another fiasco of some kind.

The craziest inmate in the KNFT "one flew over the cuckoo's nest sanitarium" had run the station during the three days we were gone. The word "fiasco" could not describe what Jack had gotten us into.

Thanksgiving was just two weeks away and Jack had put together a campaign that was running on the air the week we returned. It was his idea of how to celebrate a family oriented holiday. Thanksgiving is not a big holiday promotion time for most radio stations and Jack had found a way to change that and stir up the bleeding hearts at the same time.

When we opened the door to the radio station, the place was in an uproar. All the phone lines were lit up. We let Jack know we were back and assured him we would handle everything, hoping he would go back to Scottsdale. Then, with any luck, we would be able to pour cold water on this fire storm "Turkey Day" campaign and pretend it never happened. Jack retorted, "Absolutely not, everything will be carried out as planned!"

Nena was, and had always been the "voice of reason and picture of stability" for all of us who worked at the station. She was also the main reason for its success. To Jack, KNFT was just a toy he played with on his infrequent trips from Scottsdale. But, no amount of reasoning would convince Jack to change his plans that morning.

Jack had planned and was determined to execute a gigantic Thanksgiving Celebration. Deming, N.M. was about sixty miles south-east of Silver City. Jack had persuaded the merchants in the shopping center there to sponsor, "The First Annual KNFT Turkey Drop."

KNFT-FM was at 102.9 on the dial. Naturally, that meant that 103 turkeys would be dropped out of an airplane over the shopping center on Saturday before Thanksgiving. I suppose you can guess how this upset the liberal animal-rights-people. Jack was living his dream! We were all living a nightmare.

The largest TV station in New Mexico had leased and placed their tower on a 10,000 foot mountain just outside of Silver City. Jack had sub-leased space on the same mountain for KNFT's 100,000 watt antenna.

When the AP News Service picked up the 'turkey' story and ran it nation-wide, the manager of the TV station began catching flack from around the nation. He called Jack and threatened to cancel his lease and said the FCC would almost certainly revoke KNFT's license to operate. The newsmen on KOAT-TV did regular news stories that went out all over the state, encouraging viewers to do everything they could to stop the imminent slaughter of innocent turkeys.

The two U.S. Senators from New Mexico called Jack from Washington. They said calls were coming in from around the nation and especially from their constituents in New Mexico. Citizens were demanding that something be done to stop KNFT's Thanksgiving "celebration." "Jack, don't you understand those turkeys will be injured, or worse, killed?"

A teacher from the Farmington, New Mexico School District, 300 miles away, called. She said the school was going to load up school buses, bring the kids to Silver City, and they would all lie down on the runway so the plane couldn't take off that Saturday.

Jack sarcastically asked the teacher, "Well, how do you know which runway we'll use?" Obviously, the teacher had not thought that far ahead and answered," I don't know, but we'll find it." It was amazing how easily foul language rolled off the tongues of many school teachers who called.

Jack was well known throughout the state for his editorial attacks on the National Education Association and this was a chance for the unionized teachers to strike back. The vitriolic profanity which they uttered was shocking.

Nena and I took turns fielding the endless phone calls from irate callers. They were infuriated when we could not give them the answers they wanted. I finally began to tell them I was only in control of feeding the turkeys. My job was to make sure they were fat enough to fall like a rock. This never seemed to help smooth out their ruffled feathers and eventually I would have to hang up or transfer the call to Jack.

Jack took great delight in answering the phone. He would just let the caller rage on and after a while, he would ask the caller, "What do you think about abortion?" The caller, usually injecting some expletive and angrily respond, "What the h--- does that have to do with anything?"

At that point, Jack had achieved his goal and he would say sarcastically, "I just don't understand how you can be 'for' turkeys and 'against' babies!" Jack was giggling under his breath as he said this because he had further infuriated another 'pro-choice' bleeding heart liberal.

The UPS man showed up with a package containing a ream of paper with the signatures of all the kids in the Socorro, New Mexico School District pleading with Jack to not drop the turkeys.

The Silver City Downtown Merchants Association got together and cancelled all their advertising with KNFT. Jack's response? "The project will come off as planned." That was the answer he dictated that all his employees give when we answered the phone. And, every phone line was lit up for days.

Jack was having so much fun, he had temporarily suspended his obstreperous animosity and the low esteem which he held in his heart for me. But there was still contempt in his voice when he was forced to speak to me in the normal course of doing business.

Nena had foisted me on him as an employee. As much as he wanted to ignore me, he was now forced to cope with me as his newly arrived son-in-law. I was having almost as much fun with that as he was bludgeoning the bleeding-hearts.

The next thing that happened could not have delighted Jack more than if he had planned it himself. Helicopter news crews arrived at KNFT from El Paso, Tucson, and Albuquerque. It had to be a coincidence but, however it happened, I can't think of anything that would have made Jack happier at this point.

As the lights from the TV cameras focused on Jack and each station clamored to ask him, "Are you going to drop frozen turkeys?" To that he would answer, "That's nuts, dropping frozen turkeys could kill people."

Jack's standard answer was, "You guys need to be at the Turkey Drop and get your turkey -- the project will come off as planned."

Jack also said, "The stupid turkeys are going to end up being killed and cooked anyway, so what's the big deal, what difference does it make?" It was interesting that none of the three TV stations would run that portion of the interview when Jack told them about his question to callers concerning their views on abortion. Jack wasn't surprised, because he saw all news people as a bunch of bleeding heart liberals.

And then came something Jack had not considered. The various flying services, that Jack normally depended on to provide him an airplane in the normal course of doing business, were being pressured to not participate in the Turkey Drop. Flight patterns and routes that had never been questioned in the past now needed special permits. Jack was told it would be impossible to secure a permit by the "drop" date.

Jack informed us all that the "Bleeding Heart Bolsheviks" had rallied and were again flexing their political muscle. They were determined to thwart the dastardly deeds of this person they saw as Boris Badenov. "Where is Dudley Do-right of the Mounties when you really need him?" As this scenario played out, it became more and more difficult to discern "the good guys, from the bad guys."

Well, Jack was never one to take "no" for an answer when he really wanted something. Somehow, by pulling the right political strings, Jack got his permit. The question then was who would be the one to actually throw the turkeys out of the airplane?

Let's see, high altitude, open door, and the possibility of someone plummeting to the ground below? After a millisecond of consideration, his choice was obvious, "ME!"

Nena was not about to let me go up in the airplane alone that chilly November morning. She knew I would need help in getting the turkeys out the door and she intended to make sure I didn't end up chasing them to the ground.

It was a quick ten to fifteen minute flight to Deming. The sky was overcast and, because of a moderate crosswind, dropping the turkeys on the Deming Co-op parking lot would end up being quite problematic. We made several "reconnaissance passes" over the drop zone in order make sure of the exact release point required to ensure they hit the "bull's-eye."

I was astounded at the size of the crowd waiting in the parking lot below. I probably shouldn't have been since the Associated Press had plastered this event all over the country. Now they had no choice but to report on it to its conclusion. Every news channel was present with cameras rolling, waiting to see the carnage that was about to fall from the sky. The TV news motto of "if it bleeds, it leads" was proving once again to be true, and they were there to get it all on film.

As we made our final pass over the parking lot, I prepared to throw the first of the 103 turkeys from the plane. The first group refused to exit the plane via the window and they were violently blown back into the cabin by the propeller wash. I would have to do what I had hoped I wouldn't have to do, and that was open the door. After several more passes and a lot of help from Nena, we pushed, pulled and threw all the turkeys from the plane to the masses of people below who were now caught up in frenzied pandemonium, running in every direction.

As the plane turned and headed for Silver City, Nena and I were exhausted. We had accomplished our objective, however, and "The First Annual KNFT Turkey Drop" had been an enormous success.

Needles to say we had lots of turkey for thanksgiving that year, along with plenty of things for which to be thankful. Nena and I were finally married, all my family and extended family were healthy and my parents were looking forward to meeting their daughter-in-law for the first time over Christmas vacation.

I was sure my mother and father would fall in love with Nena the same way I had. All of my reassurances could not keep Nena from feeling apprehensive. Behind her beauty and polished, professional personality was a shy little girl. She was so unaware of her own magnetism, charisma and unique individuality. But others could see it. I knew my parents would too.

William Boyd Chisum

Chasing The Wind

Chapter 27

A Present for Mom and Dad

Jack had returned to Scottsdale and our hypertensive lives slowly returned to a normal rhythm of homeostasis. As newlyweds, Nena and I waited to catch our plane in Albuquerque. We were bound for Dallas for Christmas, and everyone around us was loaded down with gifts, and we were no exception.

As we entered the plane and made our way to our seats, we were both nervous and anxious to get underway. Albuquerque was covered with several inches of new snow that had fallen overnight. Out of the windows we could see the ground crews busily clearing the runway for the countless number of planes waiting to leave. They were all in a hurry to get airborne before another weather delay forced them to stay on the ground overnight.

As we taxied to the end of the runway, waiting for our turn for the skies, I noticed the snow had begun to fall again. The snowflakes looked like little parachutes floating harmlessly to the earth. It reminded us of the last time we were in a plane together. The Cessna 182 on that crazy day that "turkeys dropped from the sky" was much smaller than the one we were in now. If, by chance, you didn't hear news reports about the outcome of that fateful Saturday before Thanksgiving, it comes as no surprise to me. Most of the Associated Press's footage never made it to air. I think there must be a policy of not airing reports that made them look like idiots. Never once in any of our statements on air or on the phone did we ever say we were throwing out "live turkeys". We did, however, say we weren't throwing out frozen ones. The PR stunt would end up leaving most news stations, animal activists such as PETA, SPCA, in addition all of those who Jack called bleeding heart liberals, with "turkey egg" on their face.

When I told a caller that I was in charge of fattening up the turkeys in order to ensure that they dropped like a rock, it was the truth. My job was to construct a KNFT business card with a turkey sticker attached to it along with a lead weight. On the back of the card was a "free turkey coupon," handwritten by Jack, to be redeemed at the co-op. The turkey card was then attached to a tiny parachute to help the turkey safely reach people on the ground. We repeated the construction process a hundred and three times until all our "turkey paratroopers" were ready for their mission. And now you know the rest of the story.

When Nena and I landed in Dallas, the New Mexico snow we thought we'd left behind had somehow gotten to Texas before we did, and along the way it had picked up an extra element, ice. It was one of the worst winters Texans had seen in many years. And, we still had several hours to appreciate its power, as we drove our rental car through the East Texas "white out." What normally took only a two and a half hour drive from DFW airport to Mom's and Dad's would end up taking five hours. Even though we saw many stranded vehicles on the sides of Interstate 30, we prayed our way to my Mom and Dad's back door.

I was proven right. My parents fell in love with Nena. In very short order, she became the daughter they never had. The Christmas break was spent laughing and getting to know each other and retelling all the funny stories we could remember. If the truth be told, we probably recounted some stories that we didn't really remember.

William Boyd Chisum

We had a great Christmas with my family and, as we headed back for Dallas to catch our flight to New Mexico, we promised we would get together again real soon. In less than three months time, we would end up keeping our promise, but this time when we arrived, we brought more than suitcases, hanging clothes bags and gifts. This time we would need a truck to carry it all. The kind of truck you get from Ryder.

Chasing The Wind

Chapter 28

The Song of Lazarus

Back in Silver City nothing had changed during our Christmas getaway. Jack's feelings for me, or should I say lack of feelings for me, had not changed, and Nena became increasingly disenchanted with the "Land of Enchantment." We decided we had to move, and Texas was our first choice. After all, everyone knew that you "don't mess with Texas" and maybe that would go for Jack as well.

Nena started calling radio stations randomly in Texarkana, Texas to seek out opportunities for employment. Just as God had planned it, she found a job with the first phone call she made. There was, however, this little obstacle of an interview. The radio station in Texarkana wanted to see what they were getting before they would tell us to pack up and hit the road. We would have to fly back to Dallas, rent a car and drive to Texarkana and then fly back to New Mexico all over a three day weekend. This was not easy to pull off with our responsibilities being what they were at the radio station, but we wanted out of Silver City in the worst way.

We made the trip and, of course, they loved her and with a hand shake, Nena sealed the deal. Texas, the place Nena said she would never live, was where we were headed. Nena swore she would never say the words "y'all and darlin" no matter how long she lived in Texas. But she did, and still does.

By mid January we were making plans to leave KNFT for good, but even a generous six week notice was still not enough for Jack. He refused to make our departure an easy one. He broke long established rules concerning commission payments and refused to pay Nena the sales commission that she had earned on her monthly advertising accounts. He didn't care if we had money for food or a roof over our head. He was furious and wouldn't waste one single ounce of energy to meet his obligation to her. He was finished with us.

Jack would make his feelings well known to both of us while we waited for March to roll around. Those feelings were "If you want to leave then, be gone because I don't know you!"

Even a month after we left, Jack told Nena over the phone that there was a thousand miles still left on Interstate 30 after we got to Texarkana and, as far as he was concerned, we hadn't gone far enough. All of his animosity and anger was really directed at me, but somehow it overflowed to Nena. She inadvertently became a casualty of the war that raged between Jack and me.

He was a bitter and angry man and God would have to bring about a miraculous change in his life for us to ever be able to have a relationship. But, as my Dad used to say when looking at a hopeless situation, "I've seen sicker dogs than that get well" and maybe somehow this junkyard dog would too. Only time would tell.

I was once again firmly planted in the "terra firma" of Texas. Life was exciting and new. My parents were able to spend more time with me during our first year back in Texas, more than they could the whole ten years I toured in country music. We had a lot of catching up to do and, with Nena by my side, I think they saw, for the first time, that I was truly happy.

We had not been in Texarkana long until I heard about a weekly music show in Ashdown, Arkansas. The show gave local talent the ability to perform with a live band. It was a "Branson Theater" type show but on a much smaller scale. I was encouraged by several family members to audition. What could it hurt? I had not sung a note in front of a live audience in a very long time. That's not to say I had sang in front of a dead audience anytime recently either. Let's just say the only deceased part of my life was my music, along with the lifestyle that went with it. I didn't think it was possible to experience one without the other. I had already seen the worst that "the other" had to offer and I had asked God to let that part of my life, forever rest in peace. And, as I showed up for the audition, I had no intention of digging up those old bones.

The audition went well and I was asked to sing on the show coming up that weekend. I was happy about having the opportunity to sing again, but I was completely and utterly blown away by three of the guys that played in the Ashdown Jamboree band.

Roy-Dale Bray played bass guitar and sang tenor. He was a wonderful cross between the blue grass vocals of Ricky Skaggs and the comedy of Ray Stevens. Mike Morris played the drums and sang lead or bass vocals. Mike's vocal talent made him unique. There really was not a part he couldn't sing and sing well.

Chip Bricker played piano better than any studio player in Nashville and sang any and every part that needed to be done. They were all exceptional musicians. There was one more exciting thing that I found in these three guys that made them stand out above the rest, they loved the Lord and let it show in everything they did.

What a refreshing change from all I had seen. For the first time, in more years than I cared to recall, I was singing in a place that didn't serve alcohol and didn't have a dance floor. And what was more incredible was that, if during the show someone sang about Amazing Grace, there were actually people in the audience who knew what you were talking about and could testify to that Grace.

Even though I could not see God's hand at work in my life, He was busy remolding me on the potter's wheel. These three guys would become the tools God would use to bring me three steps closer to His will. God, once again, was gently turning the tuning keys of my life and this time I heard it when it reached 440. It was loud and clear, and in four part harmony.

Just like Lazarus, the song in my heart had died and I had buried it down deep in the darkest recesses of my soul. It remained there without a melody until Jesus called out in a voice as loud as the thunder saying, "Come forth, you've been dead long enough."

William Boyd Chisum

Chasing The Wind

Chapter 29

"Iron Sharpens Iron"

The Kings Four Quartet, the one my parents sang in, had retired many years earlier. As Roy-Dale, Chip, Mike and I began to sing together more and more, we decided that we should take up where the original Kings Four had left off. I think it made Mom and Dad proud that we chose that name, a name that back then represented four people who wanted to serve God. In that respect nothing had changed from then to now. The old had been made new and yet we were exactly the same.

Over the next four years, I sang in the quartet on weeknights and weekends. We all had other jobs and our ministry together was one we all treasured. I grew to love each man in the quartet, plus our sound man, Steve Oglesby, as brothers in Christ as well as brothers in life.

I went to work with Chip in the building, and day-to-day operations, of a recording studio. I joined his company, SMART Productions, as an audio engineer and producer. I also contracted my services out as a background vocalist and guitarist for other artists who came to SMART to do their album projects. It was a busy time filled with countless blessings.

I was growing in my Christian life. I was maturing, strengthened in the study of God's Word. Through my dad and the guys in the quartet, I saw daily examples of what a Christian man should be. These lessons were not only imprinted in my mind, but in my heart as well. Some of the biggest lessons I learned came from Roy-Dale Bray.

I had never in my whole life met a young man like Roy-Dale. He lived each day in a way that never conflicted with what he professed with his mouth. He became my mentor, the kind of family man I wanted to be. I learned to be a better person by being around him and more importantly, by following his example, a more obedient child of God.

Our lives seemed to finally be running on smooth ground. Nena had left the radio station that originally brought us to Texarkana. She accepted a great job as office manager for a busy doctor's practice. Her college degree in Business, along with her great people skills, made her the perfect candidate for her new position.

I was singing with the Kings Four and, in the studio at night, was producing for other artist. We thought the challenges of our past were destined to stay in the past, but we were wrong. Just when we thought we had it all under control, we turned the next corner to find we were in control of nothing.

I was once again faced with severe problems with my hips. The cement in one of my hips was breaking up and, within a few weeks, the other began to crumble as well. God's Grace is, was and has always been the real glue that held my life together, and even though the man-made stuff was temporary, I knew with God I would never run out of the real thing. I wanted to be like the apostle Paul and praise God through it all. I would press on.

This time around, my hips were like leprosy to all the local orthopedic surgeons. No one wanted to touch them. Having a fourth and fifth total hip replacement would be complicated and the outcome would be "iffy" at best. After being told by three surgeons in the Texarkana area alone that they did not have the skills to do the job, I began searching for an orthopedic surgeon who would not be afraid to try. I thought of my parents, many years earlier, searching for a doctor with a miracle in his hands. Here I was looking for another Dr. Brandon Carrell or another 'Scottish Rite Hospital.' I needed someone who could measure up to the doctor they found for me back then.

I finally found a surgeon from South Africa who now practiced in the United States. Everything I had heard about or read about him told me he was a true innovator when it came to skeletal reconstruction. Would he be the man who could piece me back together again? As I dialed a strangely familiar area code, and then his number, I prayed he would be my answer.

Chasing The Wind

Chapter 30

Body by Hedley

Over the next few weeks, I had several phone conversations with Dr. Tony Hedley's surgical nurse and surgical coordinator. I was asked to send all my recent x-rays for Dr. Hedley to review. I asked if he might want to review the reports from the other doctors who had turned me down and I was told absolutely not. His surgical nurse said, "He couldn't care less about their opinions." He would make up his own mind about what could or could not be done. I instantly liked this man.

I sat nervously waiting that morning for a phone call that would give me either a thumbs up, or thumbs down on any possibility of surgery. I was sure that Dr. Hedley could do the job, but the unanswered question was, would he agree to do it.

I held my breath when the phone began to ring. I suddenly realized what those next few moments would mean. I was standing at the same crossroads I did when I was nineteen. Eight years later, nothing had changed. The risks were still high and the unknowns were still unknown. But, I was more prepared for the answer I received that morning than I had ever been before. The voice on the phone said, "Dr. Hedley will do the surgery. So, when can you come to Phoenix?"

As I scheduled the surgery, the irony of the fact that Scottsdale is a suburb of Phoenix was not lost on me. We were just thankful that we would have the support of Nena's mother, Kaylla, and two sisters

Carree and Holly who also lived in Phoenix. They would all be there for strength and encouragement as well as logistical support.

We made our plans and I gave little thought to others who resided in Scottsdale. Facing that new round of surgeries, somehow, put everything into clear perspective. I was getting ready for a new fight and the senseless battles of years past just didn't matter anymore.

With the surgery date set, I had thirty days to accomplish everything that Dr. Hedley had requested. I had to immediately begin having my own blood drawn and saved for use during surgery. The Bible says that physical life is in the blood. Dr. Hedley must have learned that lesson well because he asked me to donate a third of my total blood volume over a four week period. I was going to give a pint of blood every week for four weeks. Each unit was to be tagged with my name, along with my doctor's name and date of surgery, plainly visible on the front of each bag. It would then be refrigerated and sent from Texarkana to Phoenix to await my arrival.

The surgery was going to be bloody and long. During surgery, a machine called a "Cell Saver," would be used to collect any blood I lost during surgery and post-op. The Cell Saver would filter out minute bone fragments floating in the blood and then re-bag the cells to be given back to me. Yes, my physical life was in the blood and Dr. Hedley wanted to make sure I had plenty of life. I'm sure he thought that my physical life was in his hands and, in a way, I guess it was. But my true life was held eternally safe by Holy nail-pierced hands. In Christ, I had life more abundant and healthier than anything Dr. Hedley, with all his brilliance and talent, could ever give me. I was safe in the assurance that eternal life, in the presence of the True Physician, was only a breath away.

Job 5:26 assures us that there will be no surprises or unexpected arrivals in heaven. The experience I had when I was eleven years old reminded me how true that was. Therefore, I faced all the risks, believing in the unseen and giving thanks for the yet unknown.

Dr. Hedley wrote an order for an orthopedic surgeon in Texarkana to perform an aspiration on each hip prior to each surgery. This procedure would analyze any fluid found in the capsule surrounding the socket, as well as any fluid that might be present down the length of bone between the hip joint and the knee. They were looking for any trace evidence of infection that might be there, active or dormant. I had been through this procedure many years before when I was a very sick little boy, but this time I would not have my dad's big fingers to cling to.

I made arrangements at the blood bank in Texarkana to begin having my blood drawn. I was told that each week they would check my iron level to make sure I could give blood that day. If it was too low, I would have to skip that week's donation, which would put me behind a week on Dr. Hedley's schedule.

It was imperative that I not become anemic because, for every week I missed donating blood, one of my previous pints was being discarded. The shelf life of each pint was only about a month. If I fell behind a couple of weeks, I would be donating one or more pints of "the gift of life" to the local hazardous waste bin. I was determined to stay healthy enough to have my surgery, as scheduled.

I took daily supplements of iron and consumed three bowls of iron fortified Cream of Wheat a day. It's a good thing I liked Cream of Wheat because I choked down, slurped up or otherwise force fed myself around eighty-four bowls in a month. It worked wonders, however, and my iron level never fell enough to postpone even one donated pint of blood during those four weeks. Strangely enough, I still like Cream of Wheat.

My left hip aspiration was set to be done by Dr. Hilborn at a hospital in Texarkana. He was one of the orthopedic surgeons who had honestly told me he didn't possess the skills needed to do this kind of surgery. I respected him for his ability to realize his own limitations and it added a level of trust to our relationship. So much so, that I asked him to take on the responsibility of doing all the testing and lab work that Dr. Hedley needed, as well as handle my follow up care when I returned home. He agreed to be Dr. Hedley's eyes and ears and relay all my test results, post-op notes and the overall "play by play" of my recovery back to Hedley's office in Phoenix. It was a strange arrangement but, if I were not going to remain in Phoenix after my surgery, it was the only way the South African would agree to do my surgery. I had no intentions of staying in Phoenix one minute longer than was absolutely necessary.

Nena and I sat in the outpatient waiting room for the aspiration procedure to get under way. I hated waiting around in those "tie in the back" hospital gowns. No matter how much you try to keep everything covered, you inevitably end up showing more of your "sensitive" side than you intended. Dr. Hilborn said the aspiration would only last five to ten minutes. Boy, was he ever wrong!

After being escorted back to a day surgery room, my left hip was prepped for the invasive procedure. I tried to lay still while the surgeon put on his sterile gloves and reached for the aspiration needle. The aspiration needle was 17.5 cm or just shy of 7 inches long. It was a 14 gauge needle with a large opening at the end called a "lumen." The needle had to have a large opening so that any subcutaneous tissue or muscle fibers would not clog it during the procedure. It was actually just a little less than half the diameter of a number two pencil. But, when he picked up the needle from the instrument tray, it looked to me to be as long and as large as a Southwestern Bell telephone pole and it was definitely going to "reach out and touch someone," and that someone was me! As I gazed at what was about to make its presence known, I remembered the decision I made when I was nineteen years old. I knew then that, once I started the process of total hip replacement, it would never end. Just like the apostle Paul, this was the thorn in my side and I would endure it until I took it on to glory.

I would not be given a local anesthetic due to the contamination it would cause when it mixed with the intended sample. This was not going to be a lot of fun but the pain would only last for 5 or 10 minutes at the most. I could handle anything for that long.

I folded a washcloth and prepared to chew on it as the long needle was inserted past the outer layers of scar tissue. I had to remain as still as possible once the needle was inserted. The fact that the needle was meeting substantial resistance from the thick scar tissue made it increasingly difficult to not move. The pain was excruciating. I had to fight the urge to tighten up my muscles because that would only make it harder for the needle to penetrate. With each muffled scream through the washcloth, I would apologize for my reaction to the pain and Dr. Hilborn would apologize to me for causing the pain. We were both sorry that day, but we both knew it had to be done. Just like all of the surgeries, and all of my mother's nightly physical therapy sessions so long ago, it always came back to those five little words, "It had to be done."

Dr. Hilborn paused many times in order for me to catch my breath. It also gave him a chance to regain his strength. It was all he could do to keep the needle from breaking off in my hip and it was all I could do to maintain the Scottish Rite 'code of silence' I had learned so many years earlier.

I opened my eyes to see Dr. Hilborn pushing and working so hard that the 14 gauge needle was bending like a willow in the wind. I cried unashamedly with each new "gust" that signified he was pushing again.

He was not prepared for the amount of, or the thickness of, the scar tissue he encountered. What was scheduled to be a five to ten minute procedure had now exceeded forty minutes. I was ringing wet with sweat when he finally pulled out the needle. He was not able to extract any fluid from the capsule that surrounded the hip joint and only a small amount from down the length of the bone itself. I hoped it would be enough for Dr. Hedley because, quite frankly, I was more than ready to get off the table and go home.

As Dr. Hilborn left to inform Nena that the procedure was finished, he paused for a moment at the door and looked back at me. With emotion still in his voice he said "I will never put you through this again without putting you completely out." It was a promise he would keep when we danced this little dance again over my right hip, just six months later.

I took my time getting dressed before rejoining Nena in the waiting room. I wanted to compose myself so that the stress of the last forty minutes could not be seen in my eyes, on my face or in the way that I walked out to see her. I did not want her to know what I had just gone through. Nena was already worried enough and any sign of weakness on my part would surely cause her to fall to pieces.

As I walked towards her, I tried to have a spring in my step and a smile on my face as if to say "that didn't bother me at all." The expression on Nena's face told me instantly that she wasn't buying what I was selling.

I had no way of knowing that, after leaving me in the procedure room, Dr. Hilborn had gone directly to Nena and purged his soul over what he had put me through. I also didn't know that he could foresee the future and accurately predicted to Nena that I would try to make the test seem like it was no big deal. On the way home she informed me of how she got her information, and I informed Nena of how I was going to have a long talk with Dr. Bucket Mouth.

The fluid biopsies all came back normal with no signs of infection and, after giving my fourth and final pint of blood, we were finally ready to fly to Phoenix. I wanted to see Dr. Hedley face to face before he got to know me in such a personal way. The only way I would be able to see him before the morning of the surgery was to check into the hospital the day before. I would need to be in my room before he made rounds that morning if I was to have any chance of a brief encounter.

Nena's mom and sister, Carree, picked us up at the airport in Phoenix and drove us to Carree and her husband Jim's house where we were to spend the night before checking into Saint Luke's Hospital the next morning. I know Mom would have liked for us to have stayed at her house in Scottsdale but that was a road we weren't going to travel because we had come to realize some defects in life can't be fixed, even by Hedley's skilled hands. The sleeper sofa at

Jim and Carree's was going to be fine because neither of us were going to get much sleep that night anyway. God, Nena and I had a three way conference call that lasted throughout the night. By the time the sun came up, Nena and I were both prayed up so, hand in hand, we got up and got on with it.

Mom showed up early to drive us to the hospital. After arriving at the front desk, I signed in and started the endless process of filling out all the medical paperwork.

Kaylla had brought a camera with her, along with an endless supply of film, to photo document every single stage of this great adventure and she was flashing away through it all. Then I was asked to go pee in a cup and when I came out with cup in hand, well, we just had to get a picture of that too.

Then it was off to the lab so I could give more blood to be tested for something, yellow fever or bubonic plague or who knows what. I tried to get them to just draw what they needed from the four pints that were already in their blood bank but, oh no, that wouldn't do. I am sure, after all the poking and prodding my arms had experienced in the last month, I looked like a junkie with needle tracks and bruises down both arms. But, if anybody thought so, they never said so.

After enough flashes from the camera to leave us all permanently blind, we found ourselves in the elevator on the way up to the sixth floor. The sixth floor was Dr. Hedley's private floor. No patient resided there unless Hedley's name was boldly printed on their medical bracelet. Hedley was king of his castle and people came from all over the world to be knighted by his scalpel. Hedley took the most difficult orthopedic cases that other world-class surgeons rejected. As I walked into room # 624, where I would spend the next three weeks, it became painfully obvious to me that Dr. Hedley and I would soon be joined at the hip.

Dr. Hedley and his wife, C.C. (formally C.C. Goldwater) live in their 8,000 square-foot home, high atop Mummy Mountain, overlooking Scottsdale, Squaw Peak and Paradise Valley. It's as difficult to get invited to one of their well known dinner parties as it is to get in to see him for medical care, because not everyone meets the criteria to get past the door. It's peculiar how you can be thankful to have been found challenging enough, or your body broken enough, that you make it onto Hedley's "I can fix that list."

I had not been settled into my room very long before Dr. Hedley and his entourage were walking the halls on the sixth floor making rounds. He was accompanied by his surgical nurse and surgical coordinator as well as a handful of orthopedic surgeons from all over the world. These "soon to be Hedley clones" were following the "master," fulfilling the terms of their fellowship.

He was dressed nicer than any other surgeon I could ever remember seeing in my life. He wore a dark brown double breasted suit that was as obviously expensive as it was tailor made. It was as if he just walked off the cover of GQ magazine. When he walked into my room, I was not sure whether to bow, curtsy or fall prostrate on the floor, so I opted for a handshake and a 'good morning' instead.

We exchanged a few pleasantries and then, with the help of his surgery coordinator, remembered which 'case' I was. We then began discussing the plan of attack for the next morning's procedure. As he used his hands to closely examine my left hip for the first time, he observed the massive scar tissue that was present from the countless surgeries that came before him.

I was concerned about the lack of muscle that would be covering the prosthesis. I could already feel the rim of the loose socket just by touching my hip with the tips of my fingers. He assured me that he would create a muscle flap by redirecting a portion of my Gluteus Medias muscle to cover and protect the new components. He seemed to have already planned for the unseen, which only added to my comfort level with this man I was meeting for the first time.

After the abrupt departure of the 'Royal Court of Hedley,' a nurse came in to help me fill out yet more paper work. It was a form called Advanced Directives, and it asked the all-important question, 'What did I want them to do for me if things went wrong?' To sustain life or not to sustain, that was the question. For a moment, I thought to myself, Jesus Christ was and would forever be my advanced directive. Christ set my direction in advance. My name was written down on holy pages in heaven and signed in His blood when I was ten years old. If things went wrong the next morning, then everyone might as well rejoice. Don't let me linger when I'm almost at the finish line. Let me go because, if I've reached that point, then "I want to go home."

That night, Nena slept in a chair next to my bed. She wanted to spend as much time with me as she could. I tried to convince her to go back to her sister's for a good night's rest, but she wouldn't hear of it. Truth was, my convincing was half-hearted at best. I needed to be with her, too.

I knew in many ways this was going to be harder on her than it would be for me. My fight would be with what it had always been - physical pain - and I knew every aspect of it. The pain she would wrestle with, however, would be emotional pain.

I had never felt quite so helpless before. Not when it came to someone else, anyway. I didn't know how to prepare her for the feelings of anger, frustration and inadequacy that, for her, were only hours away. As I watched her sleep, I realized that I could not bear her load anymore than she could mine. Maybe I did know what helplessness felt like after all.

The day of surgery started early with a five a.m. wake up shower. I would take the last stand-up shower I would have for the next 6 to 8 weeks. I was asked to scrub my left hip with an antimicrobial soap for protection against infection.

After drying off, I was instructed to place my leg into a protective sleeve that extended from my toes to my waist. This was a pre-caution against any skin contamination at the surgical site. With each passing minute, the seriousness of what was about to happen became more self-evident to Nena.

Kaylla showed up not long after I had showered and shaved. I was thankful that Nena would have her mom to cling to. Even though Nena's heavenly Father would be on her lips and in her heart all day, she would soon need to be held in the earthly arms of her mother.

At around 6:15 a.m., I was taken to the surgery holding area. Back in a little cubbyhole, I waited with Nena. The anesthesiologist started an IV and then went through the surgery permission sheet one last time to ensure I understood all the risks. He knew I did, but it was hospital policy to ask.

As the surgical nurses began to unlock the wheels on my bed for the short trip to O.R., I knew the time had come for me to say goodbye to Nena. This time, where I was going, she couldn't follow. I hugged her and told her how much I loved her. I whispered that I would see her again. "Here, there or in the air, we would be together again" and in Christ alone, I placed all my trust.

It is a good thing that Nena could not go back with me into the operating theater. The site of the surgeons in their protective "moon suits" was a page right out of the movie Space Odyssey. Hedley and the entire surgical team would be in what appeared to be bio-hazardous suits and helmets with round face shields. I was glad that I only had to look at them for as long as it took me to count backwards from ten. I've done the anesthesia count-down countless times and have yet to make it past eight. This time would be no exception.

The reason for all the added protection against germs during the surgery is complex. Anytime you expose the inside of a bone to the environment outside the body, there is a high probability that bacteria will enter the bone. The marrow is where blood cells for the body originate and, if it becomes infected, it can spread infection through those newly created blood cells to the rest of the body. Bone infections are notoriously difficult to cure and are all too often fatal.

A bone infection is a perfect picture of what sin can do in your spiritual life. It gets inside you and the infection of sin spreads to all areas of your life. All the remedies of the world combined cannot heal the sickness growing inside your very core. There is only one cure and it was not given to man by Alexander Flemming or Louis Pasteur. Spiritual healing comes through the cleansing blood of Jesus Christ and it is the only way to avoid the final outcome of the infection of sin, which is temporal spiritual death for the believer.

It is really that simple; come to Jesus and live.

Nena and Kaylla waited in the surgery waiting room trying to occupy their minds with casual, extemporaneous conversation. When the conversation began to wane, Nena tried to read a novel. She stopped when she realized she was reading the same page over and over again but couldn't recall what she'd just read. She moved onto word puzzles because she found it easier to focus on one word at a time. After five hours and thirty minutes with no news from anyone, Nena was beginning to get concerned. She found out, however, that her waiting had just begun.

Nena had noticed many people come and go that morning. As soon as they would receive word about their loved ones, they would depart and their chairs would then be filled with another group of the helplessly waiting.

Nena decided to ask the volunteer at the desk for information as to why the surgery was taking so long. After divulging the fact that I had been in surgery over five hours, the volunteer looked at Nena in disbelief. "Honey there's no way he's been in surgery for that long," she said. After a brief, but convincing conversation, Nena persuaded her to make a call to surgery and request an update. Nena returned to her seat and waited for word of what was happening behind those double doors, just outside the waiting room.

The volunteer hung up the phone. Whatever had been conveyed to her on the other end of the line was very brief. She got up from her desk and, with an expressionless face, approached Nena from across the room. It was a look one only sees on the faces of the best poker player's in Vegas. She had definitely been given information and she was struggling to find words that a desperately worried wife could handle. "Yes you were right," she said to Nena. "Your husband has been in surgery for five and a half hours and it will be quite sometime yet before they will be finished." She then, without any other explanation, turned and walked away. I am sure Nena was more prepared for, "Your husband is doing fine," or "Everything is going as expected." But, not this. The weight of those few carefully chosen words pummeled down on Nena's little shoulders like baseball size hailstones.

It is amazing how you can say more by what you don't say than what you do. As the news reverberated in Nena's ears, it was as if all the air had been sucked out of the waiting room leaving everyone, within the sound of the volunteer's voice, holding their collective breath. The realization that surgery was not going well devastated Nena. She fell to pieces in the arms of her mother as others in waiting room sat watching, helplessly counting their own minutes.

Beyond those double doors, just outside the surgery waiting room, Dr. Hedley and his surgical staff were hard at work. Orthopedic surgery is hard, labor-intensive work. It often comes down to brute force and determination. Although there are technical names for the instruments they use in each orthopedic procedure, in the end its still just nails, screws, hammers, drills and saws. An Orthopedic surgeon is either repairing structural problems or renovating the complete foundation and starting over from scratch. It's some of the bloodiest surgery that can be done to man.

I was rolled into surgery a little before seven. After being put to sleep, I was turned onto my right side. I then had my left leg shaved and prepared for surgery. Some of the old scar tissue was utilized as a road map for the new incision. The incision started on the outside of my leg just above my knee and wound its way up the thigh to my waist and then around to my back.

As the incision progressed upward to my waist, Dr. Hedley noticed a massive deficiency of the surrounding musculature. More than just a deficiency, it just didn't exist. A lifetime of surgery completely obliterated any sign that hip muscles had ever been present in my body. Dr. Hedley stared in disbelief as he looked down on the artificial hip component that had been previously inserted into the femur. It was completely visible, without any sign of the soft tissue that should, and normally would, be covering it. The normal anatomical structures of the hip were not present in my body. With each new revelation, it became more and more obvious to the surgical team that this job was not going to be easy.

My left hip was then dislocated by means of flexion, adduction and external rotation. What that means is, my leg was bent at the knee and brought across my body's imaginary midline to where it was completely off the surgical table. It was then twisted in an outward movement that separated the joint.

The force it takes to dislocate a ball and socket joint is substantial. The muscles and tendons in this region of the body are some the largest and strongest in human anatomy and don't easily allow that sort of displacement. It is a combination of strength and leverage that force the dislocation to occur.

The audible sound one hears as dislocation occurs is the combination of bone clicking on bone, coupled with a suction noise heard when using a plunger on a clogged toilet. Once the hip has been dislocated, the only thing keeping it attached to the body are muscle, tendons and skin. It is like trying to handle a wet noodle where the leg itself can be rotated 360-degrees with little effort.

Next, Dr. Hedley removed the metal shaft that had been cemented into the center of the femur. He was able to remove it with practically no effort at all. He immediately noticed a severe deficiency in the amount of bone that was left in my leg.

With the metal shaft from the femur removed, it was now easy to visualize the cup. Dr. Hedley reached into the socket and removed the cup by hand. What should have taken a jackhammer to dislodge, in the end, took as little effort as picking a daisy. The cup, along with the cement that should have held it in place, was completely loose and unstable.

The doctors then discovered a massive hole, or defect, in the top part of the socket. All the stress and wear on the socket had not only loosened the components and cement but had also worn a hole in the roof of the socket. A large piece of donated bone known as an 'allograft' would have to be obtained from the bone bank to plug the massive defect. Unless this problem could somehow be overcome, my surgery was doomed to fail.

The bone from the bone bank was, in reality, nothing more than 'cadaver bone.' Someone, prior to their death, had made arrangements to have their body donated for the purpose of helping others. This particular day, I would be the blessed beneficiary of that precious gift.

Dr. Hedley carefully cut and shaped each piece of the donated bone by hand. Once this was done, bone paste was placed into the floor of the socket, and the bone graft was carefully impacted into place with a surgical hammer. It was then temporarily held in place with two wire pins. It would eventually be permanently secured by two very long screws. I was slowly being transformed, changed if you will, into a walking, talking hardware store.

Dr. Hedley's attention then turned to the femur. All the cement was removed from the center of the bone known as the medullary canal. The femur was hollowed out to accept a new, larger and longer metal shaft. As the new metal shaft was being pounded into place, the already weakened femur split completely down the middle. It would have to be wired together in three places before they could continue.

After a marathon surgery, Hedley was finally ready to cross his fingers and close the hip. He had done all he could do and the healing hand of God would have to take over from there.

I'm not sure he realized that God had already taken over, some eight hours before. The Great Physician stepped up to the table the moment He heard Nena's first plea. His hands were busy guiding Dr. Hedley in the reconstruction and repair of His temple, which was my body.

As the surgical team started to close the incision they realized they had a problem. The hip components and bone graft were too large and there was not enough tissue to cover Hedley's creation. Headley calmly reached for a Stryker surgical bone saw and cut away the portion of the bone graft that couldn't be covered. That was that, no harm and no foul.

After eight and a half hours of surgery, over six units of blood and countless numbers of prayers, they were finally done. Now someone just needed to inform Nena and her mother that I was still among the living. Relief flowed like a river down Nena's face as she finally heard the words she'd been praying to hear all day long, "It's all done and he's fine."

It was starting to get dark outside when the recovery room nurses rolled me back into my room on the sixth floor. The technician running the large Cell Saver machine was still by my side, filtering the blood products I would need throughout the night.

I was awake on and off that first night. I would wake up just long enough to ask the same questions over and over, "What time is it?" and "Is it over?" Nena didn't leave my side the whole night. If at any time during the night I seemed to be in pain, she was right there to push the button on my morphine pump. She finally had some control over whether or not I was in pain and she was doing her best to make sure that I wasn't suffering.

The next morning I began to feel a little more alert. I was in pain but I wanted to handle it without the use of the morphine pump. I asked the nurses to remove the pump and, after a lot complaining and apprehension on their part, they did. It was a decision I would come to regret six months later.

The first few days after surgery were busy days. Physical therapists came into my room on the second day to stand me up. They returned twice a day for the remainder of my stay at "Hedley Castle." With drain tubes running through my left hip, I forced myself to get out of bed and stand. My left leg didn't feel like it was part of my body. It just hung from my waist and seemed to be dead, refusing to move. I also had the sensation that I was sitting on a baseball, in an imaginary back pocket. All the new hardware and bone grafts felt like they didn't belong in my body. It was very difficult to sit and utterly impossible to lie down on it.

At first, the only way I could move my leg at all was by using my toes to claw my foot forward along the floor. My hip was swollen more than twice its normal size and, what muscles were there had gone on strike - something to do with a harsh working environment, coupled with inhumane treatment. You just can't get good legs these days, no matter who builds them. Still, each day, I thanked God for the struggle and I thanked Him for the strength to fight that fight.

The third day after surgery I was taking short walks on a walker, outside my room. Before I left Texarkana for Phoenix, I had a baseball cap made for myself. Boldly imprinted on it was "Body by Hedley." As I wore it around the sixth floor, some of Dr. Hedley's other patients inquired how it was that I received a "Body by Hedley" cap and they had not. I told them to be sure and ask him for one when he made his rounds next time. I assured them they, too, could have one; all they had to do was ask.

The other patients on the sixth floor were upset because they did not receive their 'parting gift' as they were sure I had. I would need to come up with another catch phrase for a new cap before I returned to Phoenix to have my right hip done.

Besides keeping busy with all my therapy sessions and visitors, I was trying to learn my part for a musical our church was doing for Easter. I had one of the lead rolls as the apostle Paul. It was an act of faith to cast me in that part because, at that time, no one knew for sure that I would make it back in time for the show. They were going to do all the rehearsals without me while I was in Phoenix and then plug me in the night before the first performance. Dress rehearsal would prove whether or not I was not only musically prepared but, more importantly, physically able to perform.

I had pages upon pages of lines to memorize, not to mention all the musical scores I had to learn to sing. As the great Yogi Berea once said "It's Deja Vu all over again." I was once again singing songs in a hospital room, but this time it sounded a little better than that shy nine year old boy a lifetime ago. But could I make it home in time to fulfill my commitment? That was the real question.

What was not in question, however, was the fact that Nena was had to return to Texarkana without me. It was one of the hardest things she ever had to do. A few days earlier she could not stand the thought of losing me, now the thought of leaving me behind was breaking her heart as well.

I would be fine, I told her. Within another week to ten days, I'd be flying home myself, I assured her. Your mom and sisters will take good care of me until I'm strong enough to make the trip home, I promised her.

On the seventh day after surgery I was sitting in bed listening to music. Kaylla had come earlier that day during her lunch break to visit. She also brought me Chinese take-out for lunch. Any surgery goes better with Chinese food. Those were my thoughts that day, anyway.

I don't think Kaylla knew what was about to take place in room 624 at Saint Luke's Hospital in Phoenix, Arizona but God knew. In many ways, it was a miracle. A miracle I thought I'd never live to see. The first steps of forgiveness and acceptance in a family in dire need of reconciliation were set in motion. Its catalyst was the courageous steps of an unexpected visitor.

William Boyd Chisum

Chasing The Wind

Chapter 31

God Builds the Bridge

Jack Moulton stuck his head in the door of my room and very sheepishly asked, "Can we talk?" My first instinct was to reach for my nurse call button but I decided to hear him out. I told him to come on in. I let him know he was the last person on earth I ever expected to see. He somehow seemed different, humbled in some way. I sat nervously waiting to hear what he had come to say. I did not know what it would be, but I did know that it took a lot of courage on his part to even say hello.

Jack pulled up a chair by my bed and began pouring out his heart. He asked for my forgiveness. After more than an hour of confession and forgiveness on both our parts, God's eraser of Grace had completely wiped the slate clean between us.

Something had happened to Jack. Jack, all along, had professed to be a believer in Jesus Christ but, much like many other believers, there was not much evidence of faith in his life.

All the time I spent in Silver City, there was an element of "show" that Jack was a Christian. He had Chuck Swindoll, John MacArthur, and James Dobson, the triumvirate of Christian Radio at the time, running on KNFT AM everyday at noon.

He had his friend and pastor, Jesse Liles, from the First Baptist Church come in on Sunday mornings to do music and commentary, according to how Jack dictated that it be done. But, that was pretty much the total demonstration of Jack's Christianity.

But, God had a plan for Jack that would have a tremendous effect on his life and, that life changing process, would eventually spill over into my life in many ways.

God had sent a man by the name of L.E. (Bud) Brown to Silver City to be the pastor of a small Baptist Church there. After a while, Jack decided to invite Bud to lunch, at the infamous Red Barn, to welcome him to the community. There began, that day, a great friendship that continues even as I write these pages.

Jack had no way of knowing how that lunch would begin a transformation of his life. Bud could not have known what a powerful influence he would become in Jack's life. What Bud began to teach Jack was there is a difference between being a believer in Jesus Christ and devoting your life to serve Him.

What God had begun in Jack's life was a transformation that would lead him to sell the radio stations, become a student at Western Seminary, serve as a pastor during his final years at the Seminary, go on to receive a doctorate in the theology of disciple making and eventually create, with Bud Brown, FORERUNNER Ministries.

The ministry was designed to assist pastors in establishing Effective Evangelism and Dynamic Disciple Making in their local Church Body. It was in the midst of all these changes in his life that his life began to change.

In that hospital room that day, I looked into the eyes of a man who once was an angry father-in-law. That day, I saw no traces of that man at all. What I did see was a brother in Christ.

As we discussed the changes in our lives, Jack encouraged me to use my talents and gifts to glorify God. I told him about the Kings Four quartet and that I was trying to do just that. Jack was convinced that I should devote my life to singing about what God had done for me. I told him I would seek God's guidance in fulfilling His plan for my life.

Before he left, we had a moment of prayer together, thanking God for the chance to start over. Every life can be changed from sickness to health, from the lost to the found. Even the worst family breakups can be mended. With Jesus in one heart, He can build a bridge to another, so that healing and forgiveness can cross over the chasm. What I had remembered seeing in Jack was a self-centered, arrogant, project driven junkyard dog. The creative, clever, warped mind, that once conceived ideas of dwarf throwing and dropping turkeys from a plane, was now renewed and used to study, live and communicate to others how to practice a Christian life.

What I had seen before was a self-righteous, kingdom building individual consumed by his own arrogance. Now he was transformed into a disciple of Christ, seeking first the Kingdom of God and His righteousness. Jack was now dedicated to helping others discover the principals of Romans 12:1-2, which encourages believers to avoid carnality and pursue a transformed mind.

Over the next few years, I would come to witness the miracle of the transformation of an aggressive bulldog to a peaceful Lamb of God. The change was not only transparent but genuine. I can testify to the fact that change can and does start with His grace, His Spirit and His Word through just one touch.

Before he walked out the door, Jack asked me what Nena would think. I knew that he was really asking me, "Could this be the first step to lead me to my daughter?" I said, "Jack, what happened here today is between you and me. What happens tomorrow has to be between you and Nena. I can't speak for her." Nena was the other part of this multiple fractured relationship and God would have to be the one to bring those two pieces together.

The stark contrast of two individuals whose battles once erupted in a clash of egos, and who were now hand-in-hand seeking spiritual solutions, was almost unimaginable. However, the breach between a daughter and father is more complicated than one that occurs with a son-in-law. Jack knew all too well the debacle that he had created by taking away Nena's dream of a wedding, along with a long list of painful words and actions. If any restoration was possible, it could not and would not happen overnight.

What once was a simple statement "if you love me, love my husband" may not now, in fact, be sufficient for reconciliation. Jack's insensitivity may have brought irreparable damage to their relationship.

William Boyd Chisum

Chasing The Wind

Chapter 32

It Is Well With My Soul

As the tenth day of my hospital stay approached, I was sure I would be going home. In fact, the staff had said so. I had no sign of infection and all my lab work looked good.

I had been getting blood thinner injected into my abdomen every day. It was prescribed to protect me from blood clots and it looked like, at this point, I had avoided that complication as well. I called Nena and told her I would be flying home to her the very next morning.

I was up early and anxiously waiting for one of Dr. Hedley's assistants to make rounds and sign my discharge papers. I had not seen Dr. Hedley since the day of the surgery. Someone else on his staff was required to make most of his post surgical rounds. His time was better spent in the operating room. I didn't care who came as long as he or she could write their name on the dotted line that would allow me to catch my plane home.

Kaylla had made flight reservations for me through her travel agent. She and Jack were poised to pick me up and take me to the airport. We had it all planned, but my body would prove to have an all together different plan.

After eating breakfast that morning, I started to feel something damp and wet on my sheets. My first thought was that I must have spilled my juice or coffee during breakfast but, as I pulled back the covers, I instantly knew what it was. I also knew, by what I saw, that my flight home had just been grounded.

The blood thinners that I had been getting since surgery had done its job well, maybe too well. My sheets were covered in blood. My incision had not only started to seep blood but blood was steadily pouring out onto the bed. How could I hide this from the doctors and nurses long enough for me to make it to the airport? I had to come up with some sort of plan. It seemed impossible, I thought, but I had to try.

Dr. Hedley's associate walked into my room and asked if I was ready to go home. "Absolutely," I replied, I felt good and my in-laws were ready to pick me up as soon as he signed the paperwork. He carefully reviewed my chart and the progress report from physical therapy. It all seemed in order and I had more than met the requirements for discharge. Just before he signed his name he said, "Let's just have one last look at the incision to make sure all is well." Well, all wasn't well and I wasn't going home.

I slowly pulled back the covers to expose what I so desperately wanted to keep hidden. He took one look and said, "There's no way you're going home anytime soon." As he pulled off the bandages, I noticed large gaps between the fifty-seven staples in my left hip. It was in these open gaps that I was hemorrhaging.

After the nursing staff re-dressed my hip and changed my bed, I picked up the phone to call Nena. She would soon be getting ready to drive the one hundred eighty mile trip to Dallas with my parents to await my arrival on American Airlines. As I told her the bad news, she thought at first that I was playing an ugly joke on her. Oh how I wished that I was. I told her we had already waited this long and surely we could bear just a few more days. I'm not sure which one of us I was trying hardest to convince.

The extended week in Saint Luke's Hospital went by fast. After regulating my blood thinners, all the bleeding had stopped and, I was anxious to get home. My proposed hospital stay had gone from seven days to three weeks and I needed to make up for lost time.

Kaylla kissed me goodbye and waited at the gate as my "father-in-law Jack" wheeled me on board the plane for my flight home. It was a wonderful feeling to be able to say the words 'my father-in-law' without an underlying feeling of dread or resentment. I think for the first time Jack saw something in me that he had refused to let himself see before; strength that only comes from God. I don't know for sure, but I think he was both moved and proud of what he saw.

Chasing The Wind

Chapter 33

Unshaken Faith

Nena and my parents would be waiting for me when I got off the airplane in Dallas. It had been a very uncomfortable flight from Phoenix to DFW and, if I could have, I would have grabbed my crutches and disembarked about two hours and thirty thousand feet earlier. The pain medication I had taken before I left the hospital had faded away early into the flight. The flight attendants tried their best to keep me comfortable but nothing worked for long.

They gathered all the pillows they could beg, borrow or steal from the other passengers in order for me to have enough cushioning. Over time my airline seat began to resemble a twisted version of the Princes and the Pea Story. As I piled more and more pillows onto the seat to relieve the pain, I just got higher and higher. By the end of the flight my head was only a few inches from the storage compartments overhead.

I thought to myself, "this must be how tall people see the world." I also imagined what the other passengers around me must be thinking as they watched me build this tower of miniature pillows. "This guy has got to have the worst case of hemorrhoids in medical history," was one of the things I was sure had crossed their minds.

After the wheels had stopped and the door of the plane opened, I was allowed to climb down from my tower. I walked off the plane and up the ramp slowly and carefully. I would not be able to place any weight on my left leg for at least two months. It would take that

223

long for all the bone grafting to solidify. Any weight on that leg before then would shatter it all to pieces. As I approached the top of the ramp I saw what I had been longing to see, my family. We cried as we held each other outside the gate. I didn't care who saw or what they thought. We were all lost in the moment and enraptured by the realization that once again God had led me safely home.

The two and a half hour drive from Dallas to Texarkana was, in some ways, harder on my Dad than it was on me. Try as he might to avoid all the bumps on Interstate 30, he couldn't miss them all. Each bounce and bump sent shock waves straight through his heart because he knew shock waves were also going through my wounded body.

We were about halfway home when we stopped for gas. I needed to get out and stretch and it was when Dad came around to help me out of the car that I noticed something that almost broke my heart. Dad stood at the open door with his hands reaching out, wanting to do something. He needed to help in someway. Just what that would be, he didn't know. As he stood there, I saw that those large strong hands of his were trembling, like a father trembles when holding his first newborn out of fear of doing something wrong. Dad needed and wanted to help and just didn't know how, but he was determined to try. I was just as determined that, if it did hurt, he was never going to know.

I had made it home in time for the musical in which I was to play the part of the Apostle Paul. All my scenes were centered on the imprisonment of Paul and Silas. This would allow me to stay seated throughout most of the play. When I was required to stand, to deliver an important line or sing a song, the person playing the part of Silas was always there to help me stand and hold me up.

No one, except for the cast and crew along with a few family members, knew that I could not walk or stand without assistance. All the audience knew was that Paul and Silas must have loved each other dearly, because when Paul stood to talk, he and Silas were always arm-in-arm. I think we were more factual, out of necessity, concerning their devotion to each other than we may ever know.

As I reenacted the part in the story where the walls of the prison cell began to shake and Paul and Silas began to sing, I was reminded of how strong their faith must have been. I rededicated myself to stand strong in His Grace. Even if the walls of my physical life crumbled around me, I would be like Paul and continue to sing. This thorn in my side might, from time to time, cause me to stumble under its weight but, by His Grace, "It won't shake my faith."

Dr. Hilborn in Texarkana had been true to his word. When it came time for the pre-surgical aspiration to check for any signs of infection, he showed mercy on me and performed the test under general anesthesia. As I drifted away into a deep sleep, I didn't feel a thing. In the end we both got what we wanted, he got a sterile fluid sample and was able to uphold his Hippocratic Oath of "Do No Harm" and, I got a twenty minute nap.

Kaylla along with, the once ostracized and often infamous Jack, met Nena and me at the airport in Phoenix the day before I was to check into the hospital.

It's amazing what prayer, coupled with the love of Christ beating in two hearts, can do to build a bridge of reconciliation. 'Ma Bell' had certainly heard her share of "I'm sorry" and "please forgive me" as Nena and Jack healed old wounds over the last six months. There is no break in a family that can't be repaired by just going to the

"Manual of How To," also known as the B.I.B.L.E. This stands for Basic Information Before Leaving Earth.

William Boyd Chisum

Chasing The Wind

Chapter 34

Revised Edition II

Exactly six months and one day from the day I last checked in, I was once again standing at the admissions desk of Saint Luke's Hospital in Phoenix, Arizona. With a new baseball cap, emblazoned with "Hedley Revised Edition II," I stood and signed all the admission papers one more time. I wore my newly designed cap like an advertisement of things to come.

I was on my way to see the "King of Orthopedics." Yes, Dr. Anthony Hedley, or "Tony," as he was known to his close friends, would soon be holding royal court on the sixth floor. As I watched each circle above the elevator doors light up and then move to the next number, indicating the passing of each floor, I wondered just how many of Hedley's patients would ask him where their caps were this time around.

Recovery from my left hip revision had gone well and I healed faster than anyone expected. Since I walked with a cane, I had little to no pain in my left hip. Half of my body was healthy and the other half was more than anxious to get it started. It was as if I were driving around with flat tires but only on the right side of my car. That mental picture pretty well describes the way I was walking at the time, very bumpy. If Hedley could do as good a job on the right hip, scheduled for the following morning, as he did on the left one, then I was going to be a happy camper. I only wished it could be as easy as changing a flat tire.

The next morning my surgery started right on time. I asked the surgical team before I was put to sleep if they would try to do a better job on keeping my wife informed on our progress. "Just because my eyes are going to be closed for the next seven to eight hours doesn't mean she has to be kept in the dark too," I said. Even though I would have no sense of how long the surgery was taking, I knew Nena would be all too aware of every tick of the clock. They must have gotten the point because, every hour or so for the next seven and a half hours, Nena was given updates on my condition. She did not have to relive the nightmare of six months earlier.

When I woke up from surgery, I immediately noticed two things. First, the pain seemed more severe than I had experienced throughout all my surgeries in the past, which quickly brought me to the second thing I noticed. In fact, my realization of the second issue was almost simultaneous with the first. I didn't have a morphine pump. The written, documented medical record of the fact that I did not use the morphine pump six months earlier was coming back to bite me in the butt, literally. I guess they figured I was tough then, so I'd be tough now. This time around, tough wasn't enough.

When pain becomes more than I can endure, one of my defense mechanisms to combat it is to get mad at the pain itself. It sounds silly I know, but it has always worked for me. I was not going to be beaten by pain. I had fought it my entire life and I knew how to win. My mind would overcome it again just as it had before, or so I thought.

Back in my room after surgery, the nursing staff tried to ease my pain with injections of Demerol, but to no avail. Demerol "didn't dim-it-at all." Fading in and out of consciousness helped some but each time I woke up the pain was still there.

I beat my fists against the metal bed rails, trying to fight an old enemy I couldn't see, but could certainly feel. I tried desperately to keep my language in check. Pain can sometimes make you say things you would never, under normal circumstances, dream of muttering. My biggest fear during those first few hours of the battle was that I would say something inappropriate in front of my mother-in-law. I don't know why I was so concerned about what Kaylla heard. She was a grown woman and I'm sure she had heard it all at some point in her life but, that being said, I was determined she was not going to get a "refresher course" from me. Nena assured me over and over that night, as I faded in and out, that the devil might have control of the pain, but the Holy Spirit still had control of my tongue.

The pain in my right hip was worse for good reason. It had undergone one more total hip replacement than my left one had. That left less bone to work with and, ultimately, more extensive reconstruction had been required. The pain was unlike anything I had ever experienced in my life. I will never know for sure, but its intensity may have given childbirth a run for its money. If so, then all I can say is "God bless the mommas."

In less than two weeks, I was ready to fly home. I had to wear a brace around my right hip for a few months to keep it from dislocating but, other than that small setback, I was a happy camper.

In just a few short months I began to feel like a new man. I guess I literally was a new man, completely overhauled and ready for another hundred thousand miles or ten years, whichever came first.

Chasing The Wind

Chapter 35

Answered Prayer

Nena and I had now been married for five years. Through all our trials during that time we had been praying that God would bless us with a child. There had been a lot of what I would term "emotional close calls" from time to time, but that's all they were, close calls.

We were sure she was pregnant so many times that it must have seemed like we owned stock in the over-the-counter pregnancy test our local pharmacist saw us buying nearly every month. If Nena had the slightest feeling of nausea, no matter what time of day it might be, I was burning up the road to the local Walgreen's Pharmacy.

Everyone in our family as well as our church family knew how much we longed to have a child. It seemed like everywhere we went we were confronted with expectant mothers or women who were already carrying in their arms those precious bundles of joy, a daily visual tease of what we ourselves could not produce. It could be that they were always present in our day to day lives but, longing for what we thought we could not have, made them more apparent. In fact, that's all either of us wanted to be, a parent. That need was so strong in both of us that it hurt like nothing we had ever known.

Sometimes, when we pray for things, we need to be extremely specific. It's not that God does not know the desires of our heart, because I know that He does. God knows the exact number of hairs on our head so why wouldn't He know our hearts? The need for specificity in our prayers is only for our benefit. When we asked to have our family increased, our prayers were answered, in a way.

My brother James called from Wyoming and was "snowed in" and the company he worked for had closed down for the winter. He needed a warm place to stay, so we told him to come on over. "It's just the two of us here in this big old house and we have plenty of room," I said. And we did, at that moment. However, a few days later, Nena got a call from her youngest sister, Holly, needing to escape from a bad situation in a failing marriage. She had two small children, Reba and Robbie, who were in need of a safe, secure environment. Nena said, "We can provide that, come on." Within a two week time frame we went from a two person household to half a dozen. Maybe this was just a test to see if we really wanted a family after all. If it was a test, we passed.

Our pastor at Grace Baptist Church was well aware of our hopes and prayers for a baby. One Sunday morning, he asked Nena and me to come down to the front of the church so he could pray over us. He also invited the hundred and fifty or so people in the congregation to join us. He wanted the church body to pray over us together, asking God for that miracle that so often is taken for granted.

A lot of prayers went up and a lot of tears came down during the church service that morning. We were all sure when we walked out those church doors that God was going to bless and honor our heartfelt, fervent prayers. Well, when God pours out His blessing it's usually above and beyond what your cup can hold, and such was the case in our little church over the next few months. Most everyone who could become pregnant and a few of those who swore they couldn't, all came down with "morning sickness." It was a church-wide epidemic of "gynecological gestational generosity" and nearly every woman in the congregation came down with it, all except of course, Nena.

We rejoiced with those soon-to-be new mommies and daddies all the same, because whether you receive it or just see it, a miracle is still a miracle. Even though we did not see God's hand at work in our own lives concerning a family, we knew that His timing is always perfect. The picture and plan for your life often becomes too big for you to see and that's when you have to believe in the unseen, give thanks for the things yet to come, and then simply trust His Heart.

So that's what we did. We continued to trust His heart. A year came and went from the time our little church first prayed for us before we would finally see His perfect timing come to pass.

I was sitting in the living room at 8:30 p.m. waiting for Nena to come out of the bathroom after reading the results from a home pregnancy test. She had been told earlier that day at work that she looked different somehow. "Have you been sick?" one of her patients asked. "No," replied Nena. "I haven't been sick, in fact I feel great." The lady looked at Nena and told her straight out, "Honey, you're pregnant." Nena thought there was no way. "You are," she said. "No doubt about it!"

Well when Nena got home and relayed the story to me I looked at her and asked the million dollar question. "Could you be pregnant?" "Anything is possible I guess," she said. That's all I needed. I was off to see my good friend, the pharmacist.

I heard her walking slowly up the hallway that led into the living room. The sound of her bare feet walking across the hardwood floor echoed like a slow steady heartbeat, alerting me that she was on her way. I held my breath and prayed.

When I opened my eyes, I saw Nena coming, holding the test strip out in front of her like a person would hold out a candle. It was as if she was trying to make her way through a dark room. We had been in a "paternal dark room," empty and barren for five long years but tonight God had raised the blinds and let a little "son" shine in.

The expression I saw on Nena's face reminded me of how a baby calf looks at a newly constructed gate. "What is this, I've never seen this before? How did this get here? What am I supposed to do with this?"

I could tell what the results were instantly by the look on her face. No words were needed but, when her words did come, they were the sweetest words I'd heard her say since "I Do." With a tear in her voice she said, "We're going to have a baby."

We called our close friends Ray and Carla, and they were at our doorstep in less time than it took us to make a pot of coffee. We cried and laughed over the good news and then we piled into their car to see just how many people we could wake up. It was our own little version of the "Midnight ride of Paul Revere." We didn't have a belfry tower in an Old North Church somewhere to hang a signal lantern in, so we just drove from one friend's house to the next spreading the news. Unlike the declaration of Paul Revere, ours was not a cry of alarm but rather a revelation of praise. "A baby was coming! A baby was coming! Praise God Almighty, a baby was coming."

The day my son came into this world was one of the greatest days of my life. Nena had maintained a reasonable amount of weight gain over the last nine months. She looked healthy and beautiful pregnant and I often found myself staring at her in awe. She had a glow on her face and that unmistakable sparkle of motherhood in her eyes. This Rockwell painting scenario took place, of course, long after her bouts with morning sickness were behind us.

I had no idea that a woman's olfactory glands increased proportionately to her abdomen and that somehow it would attach itself to their gag reflexes. As our little baby grew, so perfectly knit in Nena's womb, it seemed her ability to pick up scents from miles away was growing as well. Some of those aromas she mysteriously picked out of the air would trigger an instant and all too often violent response. I tried to understand (as much as any man can) about all the changes she was going through. There were many times that all I could do was hold her hair up out of the way, while she hung her head in a place not meant for her beautiful face, till the wave of nausea moved on.

Nena worked right up to her delivery day. In fact, if some of her co-workers had not called me when they did, her eye patients would have seen a lot more than they had bargained for on that glorious day in April.

Nena had, unbeknownst to me, been experiencing constant low back pain all that morning but she refused to think anything of it. Even as her water began to break she tried to stay at her office. She was either a loyal office manager, or a woman mentally coming to grips with the delivery of her first child. She said, "I can't leave; I have work to do." Well, part of her excuse was true. She did have work to do, but it had nothing to do with Ophthalmology.

It was time for her to give birth and, for those thousands of people who prayed for it, to see God's miracle come to pass in our lives.

After the phone call to come retrieve my laboring wife, I quickly delivered her to Saint Michaels Hospital. Within thirty minutes of hitting their front door, we were both tagged with identification bracelets and moved into a birthing room. All our plans and attention to details concerning a fast reaction had utterly no effect on the overall outcome. Nothing ever goes as planned. This was especially true when it came to our son, who had his own schedule in mind and couldn't care less about ours.

He was taking his own sweet time. It was as if he were giving the old homestead one long, final walk through before he decided to move on. After nine hours of contractions coming every two minutes, Nena was more than ready for him to move on. "This is not how the literature said labor is supposed to go," Nena kept repeating. What happened to the contractions that were supposed to come every ten minutes, or eight, or even five? She must have slept through those.

Nena had taken time to call Kaylla and Jack before we headed to the hospital. They immediately began the arduous task of trying to book a flight from Phoenix to Dallas at the last minute. Once they got to Dallas, they had to rent a car and drive the remaining two hours and thirty minutes it took to get to Texarkana. They were determined to be by Nena's side when she gave birth. The clock was running and so were Kaylla and Jack.

We called my mom and dad and they were at our side almost before the nurses could get Nena into a gown. Dad took one of the chairs next to Nena's bed. He tried so hard to carry on a conversation with her but, no matter what topic they covered, it was destined to end every two minutes. She would start a contraction and Dad would start for the door. His inability to watch someone he loves be in pain extended to Nena as well. If she didn't know how much he loved her over the past five years, his in and out "dance of the helpless" proved it without a doubt. She was as much his daughter as I would ever be his son. As the pain for Nena got worse, Dad exiled himself to the hallway outside her room. I kept him updated as the night, and Nena, progressed.

It was late afternoon before Nena had reached the point where she could receive an epidural. At this point, my wife became my wife again instead of a pain-ravaged woman who seemed to burn holes straight through me with her eyes. Trying, at one point, to get her to stop holding her breath during a contraction, I lovingly cupped my hands ever so gently around her face, gazed into the red-rimmed eyes of the woman I loved and reminded her to breathe. Suddenly, and with the strength of Samson, Nena grabbed my bicep muscle like it was the jawbone of an ass and she was preparing to take on the Philistines. And, just like Samson's hold on the jawbone, Nena's grip was unyielding and unbreakable. When she knew she had my undivided attention, she then, through gritted teeth, told me in no uncertain terms, "I DON'T WANT TO BREATHE!" The bruise on my arm finally faded away several weeks later. I just praise God that when she reached out in that brief moment of retaliation, she somehow missed my scrawny little neck.

Chasing The Wind

Chapter 36

"A Brock Moon"

Kaylla and Jack's plane touched down in Dallas sometime between 7:30 and 8:30 p.m. I am sure before the engines on the plane stopped turning they were already off the plane and heading for the Hertz counter to pick up their car.

Jack could still be quite persuasive when he needed things done on his time schedule. None of those things had changed even after seminary, but they were more polished, refined if you will with a less 'junkyard dawg' approach.

Jack had made arrangements to essentially have the car ready to roll out of the parking lot as soon as their plane touched down. He said, "I don't have time to do anything other than sign my name and go, so have the car doors open and the engine running and be ready to hand me a pen that will write the first time and then get out of our way cause there's a baby coming."

If that Lincoln Continental they left Dallas in that night had been engineered with wings, they would have flown the rest of the way to Nena's bedside. In fact, driving at a hundred miles an hour non-stop, I guess they almost did.

Somewhere between Sulphur Springs and Mt. Pleasant, Texas, Jack and Kaylla saw an amazing event take place. The moon was full and undergoing a complete lunar eclipse. It was decided that, from that moment on, in our family a lunar eclipse would forever be referred to as a "Brock Moon." What they had no way of knowing at the time, that while they were enjoying the visualization of the earth blocking the light from the sun, thus allowing a shadow to be cast on the moon, was in fact the exact hour William Brock Chisum was born. They did not know that the lunar eclipse they were watching was a celestial coincidental notification of the birth of their grandchild. The eclipse was as close as they would get that night to seeing our son's birth, but that precious child just couldn't wait any longer.

It's astonishing what a change can take place in a laboring wife when the correct amount of an epidural is applied. Nena went from a very angry, "We're not ever going to do this again!" to a comfortable pleasant "Anyone want to play dominoes?" all in a matter of a few minutes.

Dad was able to release himself from the self-imposed exile out in the hallway. I think he was as happy for the epidural as Nena was. I was glad she was free from the pain as well. I wished I could fight that battle for her. To see her in agony was almost more than I could stand but I held her hand and never left her side. It was a lesson I learned from her in another place at another time.

The rest of the evening was pretty much uneventful except for a few conversations on the phone with family and friends as we waited for Nena to dilate. We kept watching the clock, wondering when Kaylla and Jack would finally arrive. I think, with the epidural working well and relieving the pain of Nena's contractions, we forgot that who we were really waiting on was our child.

At around 8:30 that evening, the nursing staff came in, checked Nena's progression, and then proceeded to rearrange the birthing room with new equipment. While one nurse was taking Nena's bed apart, another nurse was bringing in an incubator and a warming station. Nena began to protest saying, "I can't have this baby now; my mom and dad aren't here yet." The nurse just laughed and said, "Your baby doesn't care whether they're here or not; Honey it's time." Nobody had to tell my dad what to do next, he was already gone.

My mom reassured Nena it was all going to be okay and that she would not leave her side. Nena already knew I wasn't going anywhere. I kissed Nena and told her, "You can do this; It's going to be okay." I knew we were just a few minutes away from wrapping our arms around our little answered prayer. Months earlier, we had shown the picture of the sonogram to everyone we knew. We were already proud parents, but we needed to get our hands on our baby, to touch him and hold him and know that he was real. That was our heart's desire. He was emerging from out of our prayers and dreams into our arms and hearts. We were more than ready for that part of it.

When the pushing started, there were only a few people in the room with Nena. They were her doctor, two nurses, my mother and me. With each push, we held Nena up in a crunch position and Mom, on the other side of the bed, held her hand for support. Periodically the doctor would say, "Okay Nena, rest and wait for the next contraction." and Nena would lay back to catch her breath. It seemed that each time she raised up to push again, more and more people had entered our room until they were finally lining the walls all the way around. Nena must have wondered if someone was pulling them in off the street for the show. "Anybody else out there in the hallway want to come in and take a look?" is what I am sure Nena wanted to ask, but she was too tired and out of breath to care.

It was as if there was a carnival "barker" outside in the lobby saying, "Step right up, go right on in friend. See the beautiful redhead as she gives birth to the baby of her dreams." That's the way it seemed at the time but, who knows. It could have just been my dad sending everyone he could get his big hands on into the room for updates.

Finally, Nena's pushing began to payoff. When her doctor first saw the size of our son's head and shoulders he gasped and said, "Nena, where were you hiding this child, up under your rib cage? If I had known he was going to be this big, we would not be delivering him this way."

As the doctor struggled to deliver our son, the baby's shoulders were too wide and he became trapped. The compression on his chest must have been too much. This child, who had already been fighting for freedom for almost nine hours, was growing weary. The baby's heart rate began to drop and suddenly there was a sense of urgency. Our boy was in distress and he had to be delivered without delay.

With enough force to have broken both collar bones, the doctor pressed our child's shoulders together and pulled him free. Immediately his heart rate increased and, as he took his first deep breath of air, his face turned as red as the life that flowed in his veins. He let out a cry that I'm sure must have shaken the gates of heaven.

After allowing me to cut the umbilical cord, the doctor laid my boy in my arms. Oh, what a precious gift. The gift, that we had left in His hands for five long years, God now placed in ours. I handed our son to Nena and it was nothing short of love at first sight. From that moment on, I knew they would be inseparable. He was a momma's boy, and that was fine with me. He would just be following in his father's footsteps, because I was a momma's boy, too.

After being weighed, measured, foot printed, a needle prick on his heel for blood tests, and a few minutes of bonding time for Nena, William Brock Chisum was taken to the nursery. He was the only boy in a nursery of baby girls. His size told the story of his gender long before you saw the blue name card on his bassinette. He was eight pounds nine and a half ounces, 19.5 inches long with a chest and shoulder circumference of fourteen inches. He was pink, plump and perfect.

It was almost an hour from the time their grandchild was born that Kaylla and Jack hastily entered the birthing room. "Did we make it in time?" was the first thing they asked, but they knew the answer to the question just by looking at Nena.

After having traveled across the country with speeds that left everything a blur, their disappointment in having missed the birth by only an hour was etched on their face. That expression of sadness was instantly replaced with joy and excitement by the sudden realization that their grand baby had to be somewhere close by. Within a matter of seconds, they would be able to get their hands on him and the anticipation of that moment was almost more than they could stand.

I asked the nurse if she would bring our son in to meet his other set of grandparents. I watched Nena beam with pride as she watched her mom look down into the face of pure innocence. For Kaylla, it was a moment of completion. All of her daughters now had children of their own. The torch of motherhood had been passed and it shined brightly that night in the face of all three women.

I think my father had his prayers answered that night, as well. This little boy would carry his father's, grandfather's and great grandfather's first name. This child was the last chance my father had for a grandson.

245

My boy would carry on a tradition that dated all the way back to "The Chisum Trail." My son would blaze a new trail into the 21st century and the name "William Chisum" would endure.

Together we huddled around this precious bundle of God's love. It was one of the happiest days of our lives as the final piece was now in place. We were whole, we were a family.

For the next twelve months, I gladly played the role of "Mr. Mom." I took care of Brock in the daylight hours while Nena worked, then she would take over at night while I worked in the recording studio. Compared to some of the things I had seen in my lifetime, a dirty diaper or two didn't scare me at all. I was certainly not like my father who once drove for miles around town trying to find a relative at home who could, or would, change my brother's dirty diaper. I think he eventually learned how but it took awhile.

When Brock turned nine months old, Nena and I took him into the recording studio. We wanted to record his laughter, which was the biggest and sweetest we had ever heard. I wanted to have the ability, after Brock was grown up, to go back and listen to those sounds of 'pure joy' and, perhaps, one day share his first recording with his own children. I had no idea that God already had plans for that recording; plans that would not become clear to me for nine more years.

William Boyd Chisum

Chasing The Wind

Chapter 37

Deserted in the Desert

Brock was a little over a year old when I heard about a school in Phoenix, Arizona. Long Medical Institute offered a highly accelerated course in Sports Medicine and, if I could get accepted and keep up, I could attain a two-year Associate's degree in eight months. With an Associates degree and a letter of recommendation from an Orthopedic Surgeon, I would be able to challenge the board exams to become an Orthopedic Physician's Assistant, otherwise known as O-PA.

I knew I could never be another Dr. Brandon Carrell or an Anthony Hedley but I hoped that, one day, I might be able to assist the likes of them. After careful consideration and a lot of prayer, I applied for admittance. To my surprise, I was accepted.

I had to tell the guys in the Kings Four Quartet that we were leaving. I didn't understand why I felt God calling us away but I knew He was and I had to go. We would miss my mom and dad but at least Nena would have Kaylla and Jack and her two sisters, Carree and Holly close by. Brock would have cousins, aunts and uncles to get to know and that made it better for him. For the first time in many years, Nena would have her entire family together in one location. We just knew it was going to be a great move and we were excited.

I wanted to make life better for Nena and be able to provide for my son in ways I had not previously dreamed possible. There was also a hidden need to finish what I had started at two different universities but never had the determination to see through. I thought I was finally mature enough to do whatever it was going to take to graduate. A two year medical degree in eight months would end up being the hardest thing I had ever done.

Nena had accepted a position at one of Phoenix's largest banks so, when we loaded up the truck for our cross country move, we both felt at ease in where we were going, who was going to be there waiting for us, and what we were going to do when we arrived. Well as the saying goes "two out of three ain't bad."

It was late in the evening when we pulled up in front of Kaylla and Jack's house in Scottsdale, Arizona. It had been a long two-day drive from Texarkana to Phoenix in that yellow Ryder truck. As our little family climbed down from the cab, an overwhelming sense of combined finality and new beginning swept over us and we were happy to be in the "Grand Canyon State."

We hauled all our possessions and dreams clear across three states and had now parked them at the doorstep of the two people who had begged us to come, Kaylla and Jack. In less than twenty-four hours, however, our expectations and reality were destined to collide. We were about to receive some previously top secret information that had been withheld from us. It was the sort of undisclosed information that we could not have been prepared to hear, regardless of when we were told. I personally believe, however, that earlier definitely would have been better.

We got started shortly after sun up the next morning because there was so much that we had to get done. We needed to find an apartment, unload the truck and then return it before we had to pay a late fee. After breakfast, I went outside to unhook our car from behind the truck, where we had towed it. Negotiating the streets of Phoenix would be much easier not having it hitched to our modern day "Conestoga" wagon. As I proceeded to disconnect the chains, Jack came to the front door and asked if I could wait awhile before doing that. He said, "Kaylla and I need to talk to you and Nena before you go any further." I followed Jack back into the house not quite understanding his request. Had I already said or done something that had upset them? I didn't think we had been there long enough for that to take place. What could possibly be more important than finding a place for their grandchild to live, I wondered?

We anxiously sat in the sunroom, a little area off the back of the house overlooking the pool and the backyard and waited to see who was going to talk first, Mom or Jack. What we heard next caught us both by surprise and left us almost speechless, almost but not quite.

Jack looked at Nena and said, "Your mother has been offered a new job and she's decided to take it. It's a great opportunity for her but there is one down side to it. We will have to move to Irving, Texas, a suburb of Dallas." We were literally stunned as the reality of his words set in. They were moving to a place that was less than two hours from where we just came from, and they would be leaving before we would be completely unpacked and settled in. Kaylla and Jack said they struggled with how and when to tell us. Well, I think they could have told us a little sooner than when we were about to apply for our Arizona driver's license.

We left a lovely home, built in 1916, with its beautiful hardwood floors and twelve foot ceilings to reside in a two bedroom apartment in the middle of the Sonora desert. I left my family, the Kings Four and my best friend in the world, Roy Dale Bray, in order for us to be closer to them. Nena and I could not believe our ears.

251

Even in writing this portion of the book, I find myself experiencing PCSS otherwise know as Post Cathartic Stress Syndrome. I would never understand how they could first beg us to move closer, not just once mind you but over and over for almost a year and, when we decided to do just that, they were moving to another state. And, not just any state, it had to be the one we just moved from. It was enough to give us a complex. But we were here and we were staying. When Jack suggested that we just leave the truck loaded and follow them back to Dallas, it was like pouring salt into a freshly opened wound. Nena said as plainly as she could and in no uncertain terms that, "If we go anywhere it won't be to Dallas."

The news was an overwhelming hurt to our collective hearts and a heavy blow to our preconceived ideas of how things would be for us here in Arizona. We would somehow end up putting this debacle behind us. We seemed to be getting quite good at this exercise. Kaylla and Jack would move on to the "Lone Star State" and we would move on too, by staying put. This move, however, would leave us two family members short of our intentions.

William Boyd Chisum

Chasing The Wind

Chapter 38

"My New Vision"

Long Medical Institute was not a "diploma mill" by any stretch of the imagination. They didn't grade on a curve and they did not cut you any slack. If you made it through, it was because you earned it. With the heavy load of course study involved, if anyone ever got behind even for one day, they would end up being forced to drop out or simply fail. The attrition rate in the program was somewhere close to 60%. With a major exam everyday, we were forced to either "Go big or go home." Well, I wasn't going home this time.

I had decided that if I were going back to school, I would set a goal. My goal was that I would settle for nothing short of a 4.0 GPA. It was a lofty goal and I'm not even sure I believed I could achieve it, but I prayed for it and I claimed it right up-front at the beginning.

I was the oldest student in my class, by several years. I am sure most of the other students wondered just how long I would last. They didn't know that I had a stronger power working in me than anything this world or any curriculum they could throw at me.

Within the first few weeks of school, we had completely covered the nervous system, integumentary system, skeletal, muscular, respiratory, and circulatory systems of the body. By this time, we had already lost around 40% of the starting class. We still had some of the most difficult courses, such as the immune system and the endocrine system, in addition to all the hours of lab work, before we could even begin to delve into orthopedics. I would definitely struggle to maintain my 4.0 GPA.

I studied almost nonstop from the time I left class late in the evening until I started class the next day. I averaged somewhere around three to four hours of sleep a night, and that was when I could get sleep. Every morning, Nena would take time out of her hectic routine to quiz me over the material I would be tested on that day.

Nena had to take care of Brock, work, cook, clean and keep our family going with no help from me because there was no time for me to do anything except study. I know the stress was almost more than she could handle at times but, she stuck it out. Even though there were moments when she didn't like me very much, in the end she still loved me. Even in times of weakness, Nena held strong to the commitment she made to me before God. In the end she deserved the medical degree as much as I did.

When we students had completed the study of all the body's systems, we started into lab work dealing with blood and all bodily fluids. Part of our lab entailed drawing blood from each other. This was a class I know my dad would have walked out on before it ever got started. We lost a few more students during these exercises. We learned to get real proficient at needle work because the person you were doing it to, at the end of the day, would be on the other end of the needle doing it to you. By the end of that lab, we all looked like a bunch of junkies with track marks up and down our arms. But the practice paid off and, when it came down to it, I could hit a vein with my eyes closed. In fact, I saw some of the students do just that, draw blood with their eyes closed. The ones who couldn't stand the sight of blood had definitely made an unfortunate decision when it came to a career choice. I did my best to remain still, and would calmly suggest that they open their eyes, find the vein and then "stop shaking like a leaf in the wind." I found that it always seemed to work better for both of us that way.

After Venipuncture, we moved quickly into intramuscular injections (IM). We gave each other shots in every muscle from the deltoid or upper arm, Vastas lateralis or thigh muscle, all the way down to the gluteus medius. We injected each other with "sterile" normal saline until it seeped from our pores like mountain streams. Some of us offered our arms and thighs up for the onslaught so often that we literally looked like we had the measles. We couldn't walk, raise our arms up to scratch our heads and, for those Christians in the class, we found it hard to sit on our "blessed assurance."

Most schools, when covering this portion of the curriculum, would decide to use oranges instead of live bodies to practice their injections, but not this school or this instructor. We needed to know how to inflict the least amount of discomfort as possible, and oranges give no feedback, but people do. Three times a week for three weeks, we gave injections and, let me tell you, we got plenty of feedback.

Some of the soreness came from the sheer number of shots we took per day, sometimes 10 to 20 during a one hour lab. For those of us who tried to mentor the struggling students, this meant we averaged around 170 injections over a three-week period. We were tired and sore and when we went outside, our bodies mysteriously seemed to whistle in the wind.

The most severe pain and soreness came from those students who gave injections like they were throwing darts down at "Eskimo Joe's Bar and Grill," ultimately bypassing the muscle and ending up with something that resembled a bone biopsy instead. I think those students missed their true calling and could have had a very productive career in oil exploration.

We were only a few days away from midterm. How could four months have gone by so fast without me noticing? My GPA was still a solid 4.0 as I guardedly turned another page closer to the midterm finals.

As I approached the halfway point of my education, I knew I was missing out on so many other things. Brock was growing up right before my eyes and I could not take my nose out of a book long enough to see it. I tried to spend as much time as I could with my little family but there was not enough of me to go around. There were many nights I had to study on the patio of our little apartment because any lights left on inside would cause Brock to wake up and want to play. History had proved that once he was up, we would all be wide awake.

There I was, all night long, studying outside in the dark, reading and writing by flashlight. All our neighbors who left for work early every morning or those who continuously jogged at sunrise by our patio would see me with flashlight in hand "cramming" away. What they thought of me at that time I could only speculate. Looking at my reflection in the glass patio door, huddled over a stack of books wearing a hooded sweatshirt, winter jacket and blankets draped over my shoulders, I had to agree with them, I had completely lost my mind.

Midterm finals were everything I dreamed they would be. For some people it was a nightmare and ultimately the end to their medical careers. I was as prepared as I could be and, when the final test was completed, I remained at the top of my class with all goals intact.

The next four months were going to be extremely important. It was during this time that we needed to step it up and show how much we had learned. We had to demonstrate our skill levels to the professors and instructors. Our performance would also have an immense bearing on where we would be placed for our internship upon graduation. This final weeding out process would leave us at 40 percent of the class still standing.

Orthopedics and the study of skeletal fractures, birth defects along with the ins and outs of surgical intervention was something I knew a lot about. I had a "leg up" and maybe even two, over most of the students in the class when we started the Sports Medicine/ Orthopedic modules. We had to not only know every bone in the body and its function, but we had to have complete knowledge of every muscle, tendon and its place of origin and insertion. This was my time to shine and the experiences in my life allowed me to do just that.

That was never more real than when we started assisting in autopsies at the Veterans Hospital, which was part of our final curriculum. Few students wanted to actually participate and, when the Y-incision was made, the rest of the class stepped back to observe, I stepped up to assist. I was a bit anxious, but I forced myself to come across with an outward show of calm confidence. I would be working across the table, one-on-one, with the County Medical Examiner.

This was such an important part of our course that the Dean of Long Medical Institute, Fred Lockhart, accompanied us to each and every autopsy. This was "his baby to rock." He had organized this portion of the curriculum and, in the end, his appraisal of our talents and abilities would have tremendous sway in who went where on their internship. He was watching us all like a hawk and any mistake could

mean the difference between a "cream of the crop orthopedic practice" and an internship at the county hospital.

With a finger full of Vicks vapor rub in each nostril to cover up the
overwhelming odor of death, I saw firsthand how our bodies function and how sometimes, through injury or sicknesses, they can
quickly and unexpectedly fail. Our bodies are just a shell that in
the end returns to dust. It's the soul that lives on past the vale. In
the twinkling of an eye, it can all be gone. As I looked down at each
body that once housed a soul, I wondered to myself if they were
ready to go and did they know where they were going.

Our last day of school before graduation was an exciting day. I
picked up my cap and gown with its gold sash indicating for all to
see that I was graduating with a 4.0 GPA. Praise God it was over
and with His help, I had accomplished my goal.

Dean Lockhart had tried to convince me to go skydiving with him the
morning of graduation in order to celebrate my accomplishment but
I declined. Nena said "there was no way I'm going through all I did
for you to go to school to then have you die on the very morning of
graduation from an unopened parachute." I guess dropping turkeys is
as close as I will ever come to falling out of a perfectly good airplane.

The postings of internship locations were typed out and handed to
each member of the graduating class in separate white envelopes.
I wanted to do my internship with Dr. Sebastian Ruggeri who was
a well known upper-extremity Orthopedic Surgeon in Phoenix. Dr.
Ruggeri was also on the Academic Board of Directors for Long
Medical Institute. This was the "ultimate" placement that Long
Medical could offer and only one student from each year's graduat-
ing class would be accepted.

Quickly opening my envelope, I looked down at the words that read "Report to Dr. Sebastian Ruggeri." I couldn't believe it. In just 72 hours I would be assisting in surgery with one of Arizona's most preeminent shoulder, elbow and hand specialists. My career in the field of Orthopedics would begin that following Monday morning at 8:00 a.m. and, for the first time in a lifetime of Orthopedics, I wasn't going to be the patient.

Three months later I had completed my internship and Dr. Ruggeri offered me a position with his practice. For him to offer me a fulltime position was an overwhelming vote of confidence. Most of the graduating students would still have to enter the world of the unemployed at the end of their internship. They would have to sign up with a medical placement service that would help them locate a practice or physician in need of an assistant. In some cases, this could take months and the likelihood that they would have to move from Arizona for that newfound job was a distinct possibility. It was truly an answered prayer that I was able to go from intern to PA without missing a day of work. Over the next 31 months, I gained invaluable experience under the tutelage of one of Arizona's finest Orthopedist, Dr. Sebastian Ruggeri.

Over the next two years, Brock grew into the prettiest blond-haired, blue-eyed and dimple-faced boy in the whole southwest. He was talking up a storm and wanted to understand the answers to every "where" and "why" imaginable. Some concepts however, can be quite confusing to a three and a half year old boy. Our spiritual need for a savior is one of those concepts. Some people spend their whole life not knowing or understanding who Jesus is or comprehending their need for Him in their lives. You can only imagine our excitement when, at the tender age of three-and-a-half, Brock first expressed a desire to know Him.

We were saying his nightly prayers and when our 'amens' were said, he looked at Nena and said, "Momma I want Jesus." We were so shocked and surprised that Nena and I just looked at each other with our mouths open. We were taken aback that he asked that question at such a young age and, at first, the only reply we had was, "You do?"

Our hearts were pounding with pride as we watched our child searching for the words to express his desire to have a relationship with the living God. When Brock finally found the words to continue, he looked Nena straight in the eye and said, "Yes momma, I want Chunky Jesus." We both tried so hard not to laugh as we finally understood that what he really wanted was to go to "Chuck E. Cheese's" for pizza. Kids say the most incredible things and their innocence is beautiful to behold. From nine to ninety-nine years of age, the path to heaven is the same for all of us and it first begins with childlike faith. Jesus told His disciples, "Unless you come like a little child you cannot enter the kingdom of heaven." I was watching a daily example of childlike faith through the eyes of my son. He had no doubt that his needs would be met, that he was loved and it was that assurance at the end of the day that allowed him to sleep safely in the arms of his father. He knew, because that's just how fathers are and that's what fathers do. The time would come some six years later when Brock could boldly sing the words of that old Hymn "Blessed Assurance Jesus is Mine" and this time the thought of pepperoni pizza was replaced with the Prince of Peace.

For the three years we spent in Phoenix, Arizona, Roy Dale Bray called each and every month without fail. He would end each phone call with the same question, "When are you moving back home?" The Kings Four had decided not to continue on as a quartet after I left. Roy Dale said, "What we had together as a group could never be duplicated again." It wasn't only the harmonious vocal blend that made our sound what it was; it was also the love and deep bond we had for each other that set us apart. When I left for school I inadvertently broke those bonds between Chip, Mike and me, but Roy Dale refused to let go. His dedication to our friendship would, in the end, play a pivotal role in our decision to move back to Texas. With my degree in one hand and two years of surgical experience in the other, Nena and I decided it was time to go home.

Chasing The Wind

Chapter 39

New Star Shining

Orthopedic Associates of Dallas was one of the largest orthopedic practices in or around the Dallas /Fort Worth area. With a professional registry of over ten orthopedic surgeons on staff, they were a busy practice, and often in need of PA's. Because of the increased need for Physician's Assistants in the Dallas area verses the small town of Texarkana, big "D" would end up being as close as we could get to going home. The old saying "you can never go back home" was proving to be true in so many different ways. But, seeing how I had spent the majority of my childhood in Dallas at Scottish Rite, I guess in some ways, I had come home after all.

I had undergone many changes, reconstructions and renovations over the years but I would soon learn that my old childhood home with the large circle drive had undergone some major changes of its own. When time finally reunited us, neither of us recognized the other at all.

After getting settled into our new home in Dallas, I wanted to take Nena and show her where I had grown up. It was important to me that we take the time for this visit, reunion if you will, before our lives got too busy with the present and future to reminisce over the past.

I never thought that time could change this home of mine that was nestled back in the trees at 2222 Welborn Street. It was "a given" that Dr. Carrell would always be there, waiting for me to return for a long overdue follow-up.

To me, he was forever ageless and immortal. His eyes would still be as blue, and his hair would still be worn in the same way it always had. His pipe would either be in his hand or at the corner of his mouth, just above that Kirk Douglas like cleft he had in his chin. Nothing changed those things I thought, not even time.

As Nena and I stepped through the main entrance of Texas Scottish Rite Hospital for Children, there was Dr. Carrell, waiting to welcome me home. Tears began to roll down my cheeks as I walked on trembling legs towards the man who helped make the very act of walking possible for me so many years ago.

I stood shaking in front of the bronze bust of Dr. Brandon Carrell. His statue stood in a place of honor in the main lobby. He was there to welcome all who still come looking for that miracle. For parents who come seeking that one chance for their child to have a better life. I didn't have to read the inscription located at its base to understand what this monument meant. What it meant to me, was that I had waited too long to come home.

I could hardly contain myself as I placed my hands on the statue of this man who had meant so much to me. With Nena's arms around me, all I could say over and over was "he's gone". I didn't care who saw me crying like a little child in the atrium. Lord knows it wasn't the first time I had shed tears at the entrance of Texas Scottish Rite Hospital. I had paid my dues and earned the right to cry unashamedly in front of anyone in this place. All those memories came flooding back to me in a tidal wave of emotions that I was not prepared to handle. I thanked God that those precious memories of my life with Dr. Carrell and the staff of this wonderful place were still even now, after all these years, so vivid in my mind.

In the darkness of the unknown so many years ago, my parents saw this shining star that was Texas Scottish Rite Hospital for Children and they brought me to its door step, and its staff took me in and saved my life. Now, Nena and I stood in the glow of a "new star shining". This new hospital, built where the old parking lot used to be, was still in the business of saving and changing lives, giving hope and sharing love, to those who so desperately needed it.

Gone was the circle drive, the two story entrance with its three windows on the second floor and two windows on the bottom. Gone were the granite pillars set in brick on each side of the main door that I had walked through a thousand times. It was all gone, but there was one thing that still remained of my childhood; that beautiful white statue with its signatures carved in and around the base of all those who loved this place as much as I did.

It was still there, standing guard over its children like a silent centurion, immovable, tirelessly watching and protecting the weak, giving comfort to the comfortless. The statue of the women reaching down her hand to hold and help a child is an omnipotent, invincible symbol of all that takes place behind the walls of this "God sent" institution. As I looked at all the changes around me, it was reassuring to see that one thing would never change; their unselfish commitment to children.

As Nena and I stood there, for what seemed like a life time, an elderly volunteer approached us from behind the information desk and sweetly asked if she could help in any way. I briefly told her that I was a long time patient here in days gone by and I just wanted to see my old home.

She instantly seemed to understand how important this visit was for me. After a hastily made phone call to someone in public relations, she returned and said that a tour was being arranged for me and that a representative would be down shortly to escort us through the facility.

The tour lasted well over an hour. I was amazed at how things had changed for the children. Now, parents were allowed to stay virtually around the clock with their child. What was more astounding to me was that a patient's average stay was now less than seven days. How my life would have been different if these policies and procedures had been in effect when I was a child, I could not even begin to imagine. What the kids at TSRH were experiencing now, were the benefits gleaned from all the tears and endless hours of loneliness of children like Keith, Chris and myself. We not only helped the Physicians break new ground in medical procedures but our experiences, both good and bad helped in many ways to shape the world that they live in today.

As I looked at all they had now, and compared it to what we had then, I was proud of my small contribution to their better life. Knowing what I know now, I would live through it all again without a second's hesitation. I am sure all those patients of the past who have taken the time to visit this "new star shining" feel the same and would join me in saying "it was all worth it".

Just when Nena and I felt the tour was coming to an end, we were escorted into the office of Robert (Bob) L. Walker, Executive Vice President/Administrator. Mr. Walker had been kind enough to take time out of his busy schedule to meet and greet an old patient and he made sure I felt as welcome on that day as I felt loved all those years ago.

Nena and I spent thirty minutes or so in Bob Walker's office. As our meeting drew to a close, Mr. Walker's secretary entered with two gift bags to commemorate our visit and to celebrate my long journey home. The true gift that day, however, could already be found growing in my heart. I had seen this place I loved, flourish into the most unbelievable place on earth for handicapped children. I had toured the Physicians private library where some of Dr. Carrell personal affects were on display in glass covered cases. I knew those items could never be more "personal" to anyone else, than they were to me on that day.

As Nena and I walked to the parking lot I felt a breeze blowing at my back. A breeze that I was sure had been created by the closing of a door in my life, a door that had been left opened for just this day. Some people need closure in their lives in order to move on, but I searched for closure to affirm what I already knew deep down in my heart; my early years in this place were designed by a much higher power, for a much bigger purpose, than just myself.

Chasing The Wind

Chapter 40

The Death of a Vision

My career in Orthopedics was picking up steam as I worked along side the surgeons at Orthopedic Associates of Dallas. We had several offices in the greater Dallas area, but I primarily worked in two locations, the Medical City office and the Baylor Tom Landry Sports Medicine and Research Center. For almost six months I floated between surgeons, learning their styles and abilities, while waiting for the arrival the surgeon I was initially hired to assist. Most of that time was spent assisting Dr. Lancaster in the clinical setting.

Dr. Lancaster was a specialist in total knee and hip replacement surgery and, in my humble opinion, one of the best in the area. He was a big man with large hands that were well suited for the rigors of orthopedic surgery. He was always on the cutting edge of technology and was undaunted when it came to a challenge. I respected his no-nonsense approach and I worked hard to meet his expectations, but I looked forward to the day I could concentrate on the needs and wants of only one surgeon instead of nine.

My surgeon finally arrived. Dr. Virgil Medlock was young, talented and unpretentious. He was also an exceptionally gifted surgeon. We struck up a friendship almost immediately. I was as impressed with his compassion for his patients as I was his talent with a scalpel. We worked well together, and I envisioned a life-time career with this tall, slender, baby-faced surgeon known by most people as just "Virgil." For almost two years he tried to convince me to call him by his first name. I had been around doctors all my life and could not bring myself to that level of familiarity. I could not let myself slip into, what I felt would be, a level of disrespect. However, over time when we associated with each other outside the medical practice, the name "Virgil" became easier and easier to say. But never, under any circumstance, would I say the "V" word inside the walls of a medical practice. He thought that was funny, but it was his willingness to not posture himself above the masses that made me respect him all the more.

We worked together for almost two years. We grew to understand each other so well that I became his "Radar" in our own version of the sitcom, Mash. In some ways he was "Hawkeye" because of his quick wit and demeanor. I grew to understand how he thought and, by the time he could ask me for something, that 'something' would already be in his hands. As time passed, he grew to know me just as well, so it was no surprise that Dr. Medlock was the first to notice that I was in pain on a daily basis. Being on my feet in the busy day-to-day of a fast moving medical practice was starting to have adverse affects on my legs. Finally he suggested that we get an X-ray to see how my left hip was doing.

Late one evening, after all our clinic patients had left, we had the X-ray tech shoot the films to see what was going on. When we placed the developed films on the view box, I instantly realized that what I saw was so much more than just my left hip. What Dr. Medlock and I were viewing was, in fact, the death of a vision.

We have all had visions for ourselves that have died. Sometimes these visions have died because of our sins. Sometimes they have died because they were not of God. Sometimes they have died because God wanted to use this painful experience to pave the way for something better. Whatever the reason, our Almighty God is capable of taking any dead vision and turning it into something beautiful. He, who created the resurrection, can give new life to broken dreams and broken lives.

Jesus said: "Most assuredly, I say to you, unless a grain of wheat falls into the ground and dies, it remains alone; but if it dies, it produces much grain" (John 12:24). He was talking about Himself, but I think the principle holds true in many areas of the spiritual realm.

According to this Scripture, there seems to be an important principle in life that something must die before something else can be born. Jesus had to die before He was raised to new life.

The death of my vision as a health professional was plain to see on the X-ray view box in front of us. Although Dr. Medlock didn't say it at that time, I could see it on his face. The handwriting on the wall said it all; my days in Orthopedics were at an end.

John the Baptist suffered the death of a vision. It was he who saw a dove descend and light on Jesus shoulder as the heavens opened and a voice said, "This is My beloved Son in Whom I'm well pleased." However, at the end of his life he found himself in prison, waiting to be beheaded, and overcome with doubts. When John was in prison, he heard where Christ could be found. He sent two of his disciples and said to Him, "Are You the Coming One, or do we look for another?" John had suffered the death of a vision.

Jesus answered and said to them, "Go and tell John the things which you hear and see: The blind see and the lame walk; the lepers are cleansed and the deaf hear; the dead are raised up and the poor have the gospel preached to them. And blessed is he who is not offended because of Me." The vision was restored. Just like John, I was now in need of a spiritual and visual restoration.

There was no way I could continue to practice medicine with a body unable to withstand the strain. I was a liability and an accident waiting for a place to happen. Heaven forbid that my hip should cause me to endanger the welfare of a patient. I would never again be able to work on my feet in any occupation, especially medicine. I had to make a decision that, in reality, had already been made for me.

Just what it was that God had in mind for me instead of medicine, however, was now lost in deep, profound disappointment, grief and anger. I couldn't see it, feel it or comprehend it. All that was left to do was bury the vision and I did that with a simple piece of paper containing two paragraphs known as my resignation.

It had been only a few short years earlier that I walked across the stage at my graduation and had Dean Lockhart place a diploma in my hand, signifying a prosperous future for me and my little family. It seemed like only yesterday that I had accomplished so much and the future was bright with possibilities. Where did those clouds of gloom and doom come from? Why didn't I see them coming on the horizon? How was it that I could have experienced winning against, what often seemed to be, insurmountable odds in my life and then have it all end like this? I had experienced the thrill of victory in my life many times but now I was experiencing the unbearable agony of defeat. Where is the justice in that, I thought? In the end, all of the sacrifice that we gladly paid, all the study and hard work, meant nothing.

Despair over the loss of my career began to over-shadow everything. I had not even given thought about how we would fix the breakup of my left hip. All that seemed to matter was that I felt like I had been lied to. I believed with all my heart that God had placed me on this road I was on. Could I have been wrong in what I thought He was asking me to do? Was I once again adrift on the sea of His permissive will? This road that I was sure would lead to happiness and fulfillment had, instead, led nowhere. I did not even have the luxury of backing up to try again. My body wouldn't allow "a do over." I had reached the end of my willpower and strength. The life I had dreamed of for my family had now been kicked out of me, leaving me sprawled out on that elusive road to happiness, gasping for air.

I just wanted to lie there on that road and die. I sat at home for almost six months in deep depression, wallowing in my own self pity. Oh, I put on a smile when friends and family would come by and I made sure they didn't have a clue. I couldn't let them think I wasn't strong enough. I couldn't disappoint them could I? My depression seemed to only deepen as the monthly bills rolled in. Along with those day to day expenses was the constant reminder to send a payment on my school loans. Here we were, paying for an education from which I would never again have the opportunity to benefit. The irony of it all was more than I could stand. Nonetheless, I had a code that I had to live up to. "Never let them see pain or know exactly how you feel." That was what I had been taught and I learned that lesson oh so well. But, not well enough to hide it from the one person who knew me best, Nena.

Only she knew the number of times I was close to giving in, giving up and doing something stupid. An act of selfishness which, if carried out, would surely hurt the ones I loved, more than it ever would have eased my pain. I would leave my son and wife to live out their lives with the knowledge that I had given up. In the end, all they would remember was that I gave up on them, I gave up on myself and I gave up in the belief that all things work together for the good to those who love the Lord.

My weakest moment found me sitting in my car, over looking the body of water that separates Dallas and Rockwall, known as Lake Ray Hubbard. With a pistol in my hand, I searched for a tree, under which I could sit when I ended it all. I didn't want to make a mess of Nena's car. I didn't want to leave a mess for anyone to clean up. I didn't want any of my family to be the ones who found my body.

It's amazing the number of stupid things that go through your mind in times like that. Thoughts that you rationalize to yourself as being thoughtful and respectful of others are, in fact, just ways that you try to rationalize an irrational act. In my depressed state of mind, I was sure I was doing them a favor in thinking of them.

I wanted to sit under my own modern day "gourd tree" and, in one final act with the simple squeeze of a trigger, send the message that I had been through enough. Once again, I felt like that child who, so many years before, had tried to clean up the mess he made in that hospital tub, only to find in the end that he'd been discovered, naked and filthy with the mess he created covering him from head to toe. I felt the same sense of helplessness and hopelessness, searching for a place to die, just as I did lying on that cold tile floor a life time ago.

I gave no thought to the mess I would be creating in the hearts and minds of those who loved me; the kind of mess that no amount of cleaning, scrubbing and disinfectants could ever erase. My selfish choice would be a painful spot in their lives forever and an act that would never be too far from the forefront of their consciousness.

For all those reasons and more, I couldn't do it. Maybe it was that still small voice crying out from inside me saying "you are not your own, you were bought with a price, for it was my precious blood that paid for you". His voice was inaudible but it was as if it rolled in on the wind, bringing with it the most profound thought in all humanity. "Hopelessness went out with the resurrection." I got up, went home and asked Nena and God to forgive me for my selfishness. As hard as it was to confide in Nena my weakest moment, it is equally difficult to retell it to you here and now. All I know for certain is that His strength is perfect when our strength is gone.

The words of one of Bill Gaither's biggest hits were never more important to me than they were during that point in my life. "Because He lives, I can face tomorrow. Because He lives, all fear is gone. Because I know He holds the future. And Life is worth the living just Because He Lives."

I didn't know how I would live. I just knew it wasn't up to me to choose not to.

Chasing The Wind

Chapter 41

It's In His Hands

I no longer worked for Orthopedic Associates of Dallas but I knew they were the only place I could turn. I had seen Dr Lancaster's handiwork. It was as good as it gets and I knew he'd never back down from a challenge. That was the place I would feel safest. I made an appointment to see Dr. Lancaster.

Upon reviewing the x-rays with Dr. Lancaster, it was evident that I had to have surgery. What was not evident, and could only be ascertained after surgery was underway, was how much bone I had left to work with.

I had asked Dr. Lancaster if he would allow Dr. Medlock to assist him in my surgery. Aside from the obvious reason that Dr. Medlock had excellent skills, I had an alternative, much more personal motive, in mind.

An orthopedic surgeon not associated with OAD provided me with a second opinion. I had complete confidence in Lancaster's and Medlock's assessment of my situation but, the prudent thing to do is always get confirmation.

The second opinion, however, did nothing to instill confidence in the end results, regardless of who did the surgery. His conclusion was that, if I didn't have enough bone left to work with and, if they couldn't graft enough bone to make up the difference in what would be lost during surgery, my leg would be a useless appendage. The only option left would be amputation. This drastic step would be for my own protection. It would lessen the possibility of blood clots, which could develop in a limb that, for all intents and purposes, was dead. It would be useless as far as walking or weight bearing were concerned.

That was where Dr. Medlock came into my equation. It was my hope that our personal friendship would empower him to move heaven and earth to keep that from being my fate. If something went wrong, I knew he and Dr. Lancaster would not give up until they made it right. I not only trusted them with my left leg,

I trusted them with my life as well. Total hip number six was scheduled and on the books. Now came the hard part for all of us -- preparing for the unknown.

I had four weeks to get ready. Thirty days to prepare for what? I didn't know. The medical staff was busy getting their game plan together as well. We needed to know what type of prosthesis or hip components Dr. Hedley used in my previous surgery. If part of them could be salvaged, the new replacement parts would fit. The old adage "parts is parts" doesn't work in complicated reconstructive surgery.

I wrote to Dr. Hedley's office in Phoenix, requesting that all my records and surgical reports be sent to Dr. Lancaster. I would finally have a chance to read about the obstacles he encountered in the last revision, and Dr. Lancaster would gain insight as to what he might encounter when it was his turn at bat. If you know what the pitcher is going to throw at you, you have a better chance of hitting it out of the park.

I was again asked to give four units of blood before my surgery, but I decided against it. I remembered what a challenge it had been to recover from having so much blood drawn prior to my last two replacements in Phoenix. Going into this surgery, I wanted to be as strong as I could possibly be. And, I knew they could get blood from the blood bank, if I began to run low. I was certain they would keep the tank full and not let it get down to empty. One more time, I filled out my Advance Directives and Living Will. By now, I knew the questions all by heart.

I spent the days leading up to my surgery getting my affairs in order. I wrote letters to each and every family member expressing my deepest feelings for them. My wife's and son's letters were the most difficult to put down on paper. How do you express your feelings to a seven year old child? How do you tell him all the ways you love him and what you expect from him in the years to come. How can you explain to him that, if he is reading the letter, it's because you have gone to heaven to be with God and that, even as he reads it, you are watching over him?

I sealed each letter and wrote each name on the envelope and gave them to Nena for safe keeping. She tucked them safely away in a locked box for the time that we hoped and prayed would not come with this round of surgery. Now came the hard part; how to tell our precious child just enough about what was coming without scaring him to death.

Nena started preparing our son, Brock, with small nightly conversations at bedtime. This was not done without a lot of time spent on her knees seeking guidance for the just right words to say to a worried little boy.

"Brock," Nena said "your daddy is going to have surgery to try and stop the pain in his leg. Daddy's friends, Dr. Medlock and Dr. Lancaster, are going to take good care of Daddy. Brock they are going to do their very best but, they may not be able to fix Daddy this time. If they can't fix Daddy's leg, they may have to remove it to make his life better. Do you know what I mean when I say remove it?" Nena asked. Brock nodded his head, indicating that he understood. "What if Daddy looses his leg? What if Daddy has to be in a wheelchair from now on?" These were questions Brock struggled to understand. And there was one more question that he needed to know the answer to, "What if Daddy dies Momma"? Nena said, "If Daddy dies, Brock, he will go to heaven to be with God and help Him watch over us. And, someday, we will see him again. The worst thing that can happen is still a wonderful thing because, through it all, God will always take care of us." Brock understood the gravity of the situation well enough to ask his teachers and classmates to be praying for his daddy. He never failed to ask them on a daily basis.

Brock was bearing a heavy load as he and his classmates practiced for their Western Day program at school. It was the annual "Hoe Down" dance program, which was to be held the day after my surgery. Brock wanted to know if Nena would still be able to come. As Nena ironed his jeans, cowboy shirt and dusted off his cowboy hat for the upcoming event, she prayed that they both could enjoy the program instead of grieving the loss of a husband and a father.

The load that Brock carried on his little shoulders was much heavier than any seven year old should have to stand up under. But, through it all, he was learning an important lesson about the power of prayer; that when you're down to nothing, Christ holds all you need. It was a lesson of hope that I was still just scratching the surface to understand and apply in my own life.

I knew all the statistics. I had crunched the numbers over in my mind a thousand times. 92% of patients with multiple hip revisions will experience DVT's or Deep Vein Thrombosis, also known as blood clots. That means that only 8% won't have them. Blood clots, if dislodged, can enter the lungs and cause a blockage leading to death. With a mortality rate of 13.5% from DVT's, not to mention the possibility of stroke from a fatty embolism dislodged from the inside of the bone, the risks go up dramatically with each total hip revision. This would be my sixth. I knew the risks but my hope was that God had something more He wanted me to do on my journey through this life and that, through His grace, would give me one more chance to do it.

The entourage of prayer warriors began to arrive the night before surgery. My mother and father came early in order for us to spend a little quality time together as a family. The morning of the surgery, our door bell began to ring around seven a.m. with the arrival of Sandy, my cousin, who is truly more like my sister, and my Aunt Shirley, from Oklahoma.

We barely had time to start catching up on old times when the door bell rang again. It was Pastor Boyce English and his wife, also named Shirley, from my mother's and father's church in East Texas. They were just like part of the family and Nena and I loved them dearly.

Prior to heading to the hospital, we all joined hands in our living room and gave thanks to God in advance, not knowing what His will would be, but understanding that, whatever the outcome, in our hearts on that day, God would get the glory.

After checking into Baylor, my little group of Christian soldiers marched on up to the third floor and together we waited for me to be called back to surgery holding. Nena's mom, Kaylla, met us there shortly after we arrived. After our experiences in Phoenix eleven years earlier, she was a pro at warming a surgery waiting room chair.

Nena and I had explained to Brock in great detail just how this day would unfold. He had brought along his backpack filled with coloring books, a Game Boy and a multitude of play things to help keep his mind off all those questions that no one seemed to be able to answer. But, if you took the time to look deep in his beautiful blue eyes, you could see his thoughts were not on his toys.

There weren't enough seats for all of us to sit together so, we sat next to strangers and got to know their needs and who and what brought them to this room for the helplessly waiting. As we waited for my named to be called, I noticed that my cousin, Sandy, was crying. I left Nena's side and sat down with her and we prayed together. She was so worried and, as I tried to comfort her, my Aunt Shirley joined us. In tearful harmony they "let them roll" so I passed her some Kleenex as well. Just as I thought I had those leeks stopped, I looked up and saw that Sandy had moved over by my mom and they, too, decided to start crying. I began to feel like the little Dutch boy trying to stop all the leaks in the dam. In their tears, I know they we showing me how much they loved me and how much they all wanted things to work out right.

As I watched my son play at my feet and held my wife's hand, I looked around me and felt a peaceful calm assurance. I was surrounded by those who loved me and, in the end, I could never ask for more in my life than that. Then God gave me that little something extra that He always does. I looked up and, standing in front of me, was my brother in Christ and my friend for life, Roy Dale Bray. He had told me he would try to come but I wasn't sure he would make it. I stood and wrapped my arms around the man who was and still is my spiritual mentor. We were all there and we were all ready for the fight. Whatever my lot was to be at the end of that day, I knew one thing without a shadow of a doubt, it was well with my soul.

"William Boyd Chisum," the nurse's voice rang out like an alarm clock, waking us all from a self-induced mental slumber, alerting us that it was time for me to go. Everyone lined up, like at a wedding reception, in order to give me their last bits of encouragement. The nurse waited patiently for me to work my way through the "receiving line," and then Nena and Brock followed me into surgery holding. I was put into a gown and a needle was securely placed in my arm. I noticed that Brock could not watch me undergo that procedure, "A genetic flaw that he must have inherited from his grandpa," I thought to myself. I sure hoped that Brock got his hair follicle genes from his momma's side because grandpa didn't have any.

As we waited, I saw many familiar faces as hospital staff walked by and waved or said hello. They were employees of Baylor Hospital and other PA's from OAD that I had worked with before. It was awkward to have them see me like this. I knew, however, that they were about to see a lot more of me than I ever, in a million years, intended them to see.

Dr. Lancaster stopped by to let me know that they were getting things ready in the surgery theater and that they would call for me to be brought back in thirty minutes or so. A practiced pre-surgical protocol speech that I had heard a million times before.

By now, my dad and mom had somehow convinced the nursing staff to allow them to join us in surgery holding. I asked my dad to escort Brock back out into the waiting room where Sandy could keep an eye on him. I did not want him to see them take me away.

He shouldn't have to replay that memory over and over in his mind if today did not go well, I thought. He reached out and hugged me, this child I loved with all my heart, and I reassured him that it would all be okay. He gave me a kiss and a forced smile and he was gone, but I knew I would see him again. Here, there or in the air, I would see my "little man" again.

Dr. Medlock finally came running through on his way to scrub in. He had been in clinic all morning. Liz, his surgery scheduler, had blocked off the rest of his day just for me. "Are you ready" Dr. Medlock asked? "Are you ready?" I replied. "We have everything, including the kitchen sink, waiting in OR. We are ready for anything!" he said. "We barely have room to turn around because of the three tables of replacement hardware from multiple companies and vendors." If my hip could be fixed they were making sure they had enough stuff to do it with.

As Dr. Medlock started to leave he paused and looked at me and said, "Remember, our job is to do our best and we will. Your job, and the only one you have today, is to wake up." I understood what he meant but I had already subcontracted that job into the hands of someone else; hands that have done that job for me all of my life.

With Dr. Medlock's departure, a nurse came to give me what I have always referred to as my "don't give a damn shot"; but clinically known as Versed. A powerful medication placed into my IV in order to relax me. She said "in a few short minutes you won't remember what's been said so you might think about saying goodbye to your family now." I gave my mom and dad a hug and asked my dad to take care of Nena. I knew he would, but I had to ask. Nena leaned over and gave me a goodbye kiss. She was trying so hard not cry. She was being strong for me. She didn't want her tears to be the last thing I saw on her face in case God had other plans for our future. I told her I loved her and, as they started to wheel me away, I turned around to look at her one last time. My dad has already stepped up to do his job. He had his strong arms wrapped around Nena's shoulders, where I knew they would stay until this day was behind us.

As we approached the surgery room I heard a familiar voice, "You mind if I walk the rest of the way with you?" the voice asked. I turned to see Pam Gamble, Dr. Lancaster's PA, coming out from where she had been putting on her scrubs. She had been a good friend to me during the two years I worked at OAD. She reached out and took my hand as I said, "Sure I'd love for you to join me." The medication I had been given suddenly took effect. I don't remember anything after that. The memory control portion of my brain had been turned off, like turning off a light switch. My consciousness faded into oblivion.

The mist coming up from the oxygen mask made it hard for me to see. I heard a nurse telling me as she took my vital signs, "keep your eyes open Boyd, you're in recovery now, it's all over." Fading in and fading out again I tried to wake up long enough to find the answer. Each time I woke up it seemed like hours had gone by when in all actuality it was but a few seconds. Did I look last time I opened my eyes or didn't I? Was it there or wasn't it? I couldn't remember. Coming out of the confusion brought on by the anesthesia, left everything uncertain. I wasn't even sure of where I was.

Finally I was able to formulate a thought long enough to act on it. I needed to look down to the end of the bed to see what kind of outline my body made under the sheets. Try as might I couldn't see past my chest. I knew about "phantom pain" that amputees experience. I understood that the pain I had in my left leg at that moment did not mean that in fact I still had a left leg.

Oh, but even in the midst of all the uncertainty I was still so thankful to be alive. Thankful to God that I would get to see my son grow up and that I had been given more time with my wife and family that I loved so much. God had granted me another chance to serve Him and seek a new vision. How would I spend that time? Would I be standing on my "own two feet" or rolling through life in a chair? How much was left of me? I had to know and I had to know right then.

I didn't have the strength to set up so I turned my head to the left side and clawed at the sheets with my fingers until I had enough of it in my hand to pull it away. I pulled the corner of the sheet back just enough to see. Through the mist of the mask, I got my answer. I let the covers fall where they may and I cried.

William Boyd Chisum

Chasing The Wind

Chapter 42

Grace Still Amazing

In the surgery waiting area our not so little support team had decided it was time to have lunch. They knew that no news would be forth coming for many hours. They filed out leaving Nena and her mom behind. Roy Dale decided to stay by Nena's side as well. Nena was not in the mood for conversation anyway and the added pressure of entertaining our guests was something she no longer had the strength for. She just wanted to sit quietly, wait and pray.

After a while all the family and friends returned and they took up where they had left off. They were Nena and Brock's "prop up team for a day" and they were back doing their job.

After a quick lunch, Nena and Kaylla with Brock in tow returned to the waiting room to find still no news. Brock played his Game Boy and colored. The men made frequent trips down stairs and this gave Brock an opportunity to burn off the kind of nervous energy that can only be found in a seven year old boy. The walks were designed more for the preoccupation of a frightened little child than exercise for the adults that instigated them. It also was a way to help take a little load off Nena as well.

Finally the surgery updates began to come in. Nothing more than "the surgery is going well" or "Boyd is doing fine" but it was information that they needed to hear. After five and a half hours the one call they had been waiting for finally came. "Boyd's out of surgery and they have requested that the family wait up stairs for a conference with Dr. Lancaster" said the waiting room nurse.

It seemed like a long wait but finally the surgeons appeared from around the corner. Dr. Lancaster looking huge and stern followed by Dr. Medlock who had the expression of the "Cheshire cat that just ate the canary" on his face. His look instantly gave it away, they had accomplished all they had set out to do, and in six months I would be standing on "my own two legs". It was all they had been praying for and once again Gods Amazing Grace amazes all.

The family then gathered for a prayer of thanks led by Bro. Boyce English. The day was gone and with darkness already beginning to fall everyone decided it was time to head for home, everyone but Nena, Kaylla and Roy Dale. Kaylla told Nena that she wasn't leaving until she laid eyes on me. "Seeing is believing" and in a way they all three needed to see with their own eyes. Nena wasn't going home that night anyway. She would sleep in a chair by my side.

Roy Dale refused to leave as well and opted to sleep in his van down in the parking lot, but not before giving Nena his cell number. "If you need me I can be up here in a few minutes" was the unspoken message from Roy Dale to Nena. I am only a parking lot away.

With plans made for the night they all waited for me to come up from recovery. They waited and they waited. What was keeping them in recovery? Nena finally had a nurse call the recovery room to find out what was wrong. She relayed the news that they were waiting for me to be cleared to come to the floor. They waited a while longer and the nurse put in another call to recovery. "Mrs. Chisum, you will receive a call in the room your husband is going to in just a short while" the nurse said. So the "three remaining musketeers" moved into my room and waited.

The time came and went and the call didn't come. Several times Nena picked up the phone to see if it was working, it was. Something had gone wrong from the time that Dr. Lancaster informed the family and now, something that no one was talking about. Nena knew it in her heart but it was what she didn't know that was causing it to break.

I kept asking the recovery nurse what was taking so long. Why wasn't I being allowed to go to my room? We need to get an x-ray of your lungs she said. I had noticed that it had become harder for me to breath and that there was a "wheezing" sound coming from inside my chest. The combination of the need for an x-ray and the chest sounds instantly told me what they were looking for, a pulmonary embolism.

Had I thrown a blood clot that had lodged itself in one of my lungs? That would explain the sense of urgency in the medical staffs request as well as my extended stay in recovery. All I could do was wait as they searched for the radiologist to read the films.

The nurses tried to keep me comfortable with medication to ease the pain, but the medication I was in dire need of, was waiting for me in my room. Three more hours go by and I finally couldn't stand it any longer. I ask the nurse if she could call my room so I could speak to my wife. I needed to let her know what was going on. I needed to hear her voice. She dialed my room number on her wireless phone and before the first ring could finish Nena frantically said hello.

It was hard to hear her over the hissing sound that the oxygen mask created but I could hear enough. I tried to fill Nena in on what I knew about my condition. I told her I loved her and that I hoped I would see her soon. With a goodbye I handed the phone back to the nurse feeling a hundred percent better than I had just a few minutes before.

At the end of the day the diagnosis was that I had fluid build up in my lungs and around my heart. It was a condition they would have to keep a close eye on over the days to come but for right now I was stable enough to leave recovery.

Five and a half hours of surgery and over three and half hours in recovery and finally Praise be to God this day was coming to an end.

William Boyd Chisum

Chasing The Wind

Chapter 43

Bowling for Boyd

On that 25th of March, across the whole United States, there were hundreds of people praying. They were praying that God would do a mighty work in my life one more time. Churches in several different countries, as well, had placed my needs on their lips.

It is a humbling thing to realize that so many people would take the time out of their own daily struggles to approach the throne of God in prayer on your behalf. Prayer works and I was thankful to all those unknown, unseen prayer warriors who lifted me up to the Throne of Grace.

One of the most unique examples of that took place with a group of more than thirty individuals in the little town of Sequin, Texas. They had planned a night out together called "Bowling for Boyd". This group of my old high school friends, led by Dave and Kelly Dickey and their children, huddled together in support and prayer in a bowling alley. They reminisced about our high school days and made a commitment to keep bowling until Kelly's cell phone brought news that it was over. When Nena made her first few phone calls with the good news, it started a chain reaction of rings. When Dave and Kelly's turn came up in this endless relay of calls, you would have thought someone had just bowled a perfect game. The cheers went up throughout the place as news spread from lane to lane like pins being knocked down for a strike.

Somewhere between the pins and the gutters and all those funny looking shoes, our mighty God heard their plea's and allowed each person there to experience the revelation that prayer works.

William Boyd Chisum

Chasing The Wind

Chapter 44

Lay Your Burden Down

"Come to me, all who are weary
Come to me and rest can be found
Come you'll find peace for your trouble soul
Just come and lay your burden down."

The inspiration for the words to this song came straight from the mouth of Jesus Christ Himself in (Matt. 11:28-29). He's pleading for us to drop the load of heavy burdens, like stones around our neck that we carry around every day and, instead, take up His load for it is light and easy to bear.

But for many of us, we just can't seem to lay them down. We hold onto the stones of stress, rocks of regret, and rocks of rejection. Some of us cling to the boulders of betrayal but, regardless of what name we give it, all that extra baggage causes us to fall face down on the road of life. From time-to-time, however, we may allow those stones to roll out of our grasp, for others to see. It's an opportunity to pray over what we're going through, and ask for deliverance from the load we are under. But then, when all is said and done, we get up off our knees, gather up our rocks and continue to carry the heavy load.

We continue to stumble down life's road until we come to another failure, another stone in the road. We pick it up and add to our collection. We become so accustomed to being bent over from the heavy load that we take solace in it. The contortion of our body and spirit make it easier to pick up the next stone, whether it's truly ours to carry or not. So on we go, collecting stones for this necklace of regret.

When the storms of life roll in and the water begins to rise, we fight the tide rising against us only to find it impossible to stay a float. Those very same mill stones, which we placed around our necks, begin to slowly pull us down until we feel suffocated. The burden becomes too much to bear and we give in and give up.

As I lay in my bed at home, after a week in the hospital, I wondered, "What is it God wants me to see through His Eyes when He looks at me?" I thought of all the stones I had carried around in my life. Those stones, at times, had become so large that they changed my perspective of who I was and what I was. Stones that caused me to make decisions about my life that, in the end, led me further from the One who waited patiently to chisel His vision for my life out of those very same stones.

His goal was, and still is, to chisel away everything in my life that doesn't conform to the image of Christ. That's what He wants me to see, when I see myself through His perfect vision of grace. So, in the end, it took a cataclysmic avalanche to bring about the death of my vision of me, in order for me to start seeking His vision of me.

I started searching for the Genesis of a new vision, Gods vision for my life. The first steps toward that began when I realized that "He Still Moves the Stone" and no matter how much pressure I had gone through, God never allowed me to be crushed.

Throughout my life there were times I had been broken, beaten, powerless and helpless but never through any of it was I ever hopeless, because there is no place for the word hopeless in the vocabulary of a believer.

In 2 Cor. 4:7-10 it says:
"But we have this treasure in earthen vessels, that the excellence of the power may be of God and not of us. We are hard-pressed on every side, yet not crushed; we are perplexed, but not in despair; persecuted, but not forsaken; struck down, but not destroyed, always carrying about in the body the dying of the Lord Jesus, that the life of Jesus also may be manifested in our body."

This passage from the Apostle Paul's letter to the Corinthians transcends all time and space. The letter went to the Christians in Corinth but God knew the message was also meant for me. If I were to ever find God's image of me waiting "dormant and formless in the stone," I would have to begin with the understanding and application of this principal to my life. The hammer came down on the chisel and, in one mighty blow, the stone slowly began to take shape.

Chasing The Wind

Chapter 45

Symphony of Grace

The moon was created to shine in the night and illuminate the darkness. The sun was created to shine in the day, providing warmth and creating the process of photosynthesis therefore allowing plants and all living things oxygen to grow. The sun does not try to shine in the darkness of the night nor does the moon cast its illumination on the day. They were created by God for their own specific purpose. Two separate sections in a symphony of His creation. The bigger purpose of each section of the symphony was so that man could see the greatness of the conductor, the Alpha and Omega as He alone interprets the ebb and flow, when and where each one comes in and fades out.

As I studied God's Word, I found that, in some ways, we are no different than the stars, the sun and the moon. Each of us is a unique creation. We have exclusive, specific, talents and are endowed at the very moment of conception with a single purpose and that purpose is to have a relationship with the One who was, is and always will be the living God, through Christ Jesus, His son. With the rebirth through Christ comes the conversion of our talents to spiritual gifts as we offer them for His glory. Fellowship with Christ is the ultimate goal through spiritual growth but it can't take place without first having a relationship.

It wasn't hard for me to break down all those gifts in my life that God Had given me. As I looked, I saw they all revolved around a melody, and a song. What we choose to do with those gifts He has given us will, in the end, determine the rewards we receive for what we do with those gifts.

While I recovered from the miracle of JEHOVA-ROPHE (Hebrew for "The Lord who heals"), I sought diligently to hear God's voice speak to me through the pages of His written Word. If all of this pain and heartache I had gone through was to somehow bring me to this point in my life, then I was not going to move away from it until I received what it was He wanted me to have.

What I realized is that God had been trying to compose this master piece of music, a "Regal Requiem of Grace" for me to sing for His glory, not mine. Oh, there were times in my life when I gave a nod to God for the song I was singing but, sadly, too often I kept Him hidden back stage, behind the curtain so I could take the bow.

I had never understood until now that God had provided for me an Orchestra in my life that consisted of seven sections. But, I had not allowed Him to fully develop those sections in my soul so His symphony could be heard loud and clear.

That's why the music of my life never sounded the way God intended. The Conductor of my life had, all too often, pointed his baton at sections that just weren't ready to play, were out of tune or were too busy playing a different melody to pay attention.

In 2 Peter 1:5-7, the apostle, in essence, is saying that in order for us to be able to enjoy God's full Philharmonic Orchestra in our lives, we need to be hearing all seven sections playing as one, a united chorus.

Peter used a word in the original language of that day that brought a musical connotation to the application of what he was saying.

From the original word that Peter used, we get our modern English word "chorus."

To emphasize this unique application of Peter's use of a musical term, Kenneth Gangel, Distinguished Professor Emeritus of Christian Education at Dallas Theological Seminary in, The New Testament section of The Bible Knowledge Commentary on pages 859-879 said,

"In this beautiful paragraph Peter orchestrates a symphony of grace. To the melody line of faith he leads believers to add harmony in a blend of seven Christian virtues which he lists without explanation or description."

Peter said, "But also for this very reason, giving all diligence, add to your faith virtue, to virtue knowledge, to knowledge self-control, to self-control perseverance, to perseverance godliness, to godliness brotherly kindness, and to brotherly kindness love.

So, these seven symphonic sections are 1) virtue, 2) knowledge, 3) self-control, 4) perseverance, 5) godliness, 6) brotherly kindness, and 7) love.

Sometimes those seven sections were absent altogether in my life, leaving a silence that was far from golden in the melody He had written for me. I needed to learn and apply these seven missing parts; parts from a score that was written on my soul by the "Preeminent Virtuoso of Love," the Lord Jesus Christ.

Peter had followed Jesus around for about three years, so it should not seem unusual that Peter would say things that closely resemble the things that Jesus taught.

The first thing Peter said we should add to our faith is "virtue" and he had just used this same word in verse three to describe the character of Christ. There is no greater virtue than the divine nature of Christ.

The first part or section that needs to be present in our lives is adding to our faith through the living Word. The living Word is Jesus Christ in us. The daily evaluation of where we are as in comparison to the character of Christ Jesus.

Jesus gave us instructions in Luke 14:26-33 that suggest we are to strive daily to draw so near to God that we can actually tell when our life is in tune with His will. To do that, we must be willing to put Jesus first, above all relationships and all things or possessions. Then, we have to be willing to listen and analyze daily whether we've fallen a few milliseconds sharp or flat as it relates to God's tuning for our life. But we should all understand that there's a price to pay when we put Jesus first; it'll cost everything. But if we do, the benefits will mean so much more. "To loose it all, to gain it all and count it all but loss for my King, It'll cost everything".

Part two is comprised of spiritual knowledge. Peter said that we need to add to our faith, "knowledge." In John 8:31-32, Jesus said abide in my Word. We should daily engage in a careful systematic Bible study led by the Holy Spirit and allow Him to guide our lives by what we discover in it. Paul said "be diligent to present yourself to God, a worker who does not need to be ashamed, rightly dividing the Word of truth." A Christian should always be making progress on a daily basis in his or her spiritual growth.

If a man only knows how to play one chord can he write a symphony? God speaks through His Word and we grow through the mental consumption and spiritual application of that written Word.

Most of us know about the beginning of the Bible and have some understanding of how it all ends, but the good stuff, the stuff most of us miss, the "blue print, the building blocks for life stuff" is found in between. We need to get in The Book, stay in The Book, and let the message of The Book live in us.

In section three of the orchestra, Peter said we are to add to our faith, "self-control" and this is one that most of us struggle with on an hourly basis. The seats to that section of God's symphony for our life are all too often empty. In Luke 9:23 Jesus put it like this, "deny self."

When we believed in Jesus Christ we receive a "new nature." We are a new creation and our sins are washed away but our old sin nature doesn't just disappear. The difference is we should no longer want to pursue that old sin nature. That doesn't, however, mean that the old sin nature does not want to pursue us. And now, when we give in to our old nature, something divine takes place. We become convicted by the Holy Spirit.

Satan is still up to his old dirty tricks. He uses the terrible trio of lust of the flesh, lust of the eyes, and pride of life, to start a battle between our new nature and the old. We need to learn how to depend on God's strength and direction to help us win those battles. It is a choice we make, consciously or subconsciously, everyday. Whose voice do we hear speaking in the ear of our conscience?

When I was ten years old, my mother and father tried, for what seemed like weeks, to teach me to sing harmony. Dad would sing the lead or melody and mom would sing the part I was supposed to sing. I could sing and follow along with her but, when she moved to her own harmony line and left me to carry my own part, I got lost. Because I could hear the melody so much clearer than the harmony, it was easy for me to slide back into the melody. Sliding back and forth from harmony to melody, from Christ centered to self centered, creates a tune that can't be sung and music that can't be appreciated.

God says we need to ignore our old sin nature. When our first impulse is to sing the lead, to be self centered, we have to stop and listen. We have to be one or the other, because no one can be both.

In section Four, Peter said we are to add to our faith 'perseverance' and that is designed to encourage the Christian to "press on." Jesus said we are to 'take up our cross and follow him daily.' The message of Matthew 16:24 is tantamount to saying that we are to make Jesus Lord of our life. We are to submit to God's will for our lives everyday.

Just like many others, I spent years of my life chasing the wind. It was hard to let go of the tight grip I had on my life and place it in nail pierced hands when I was so sure that my plan was better than one that anyone else could have.

I have dragged my guitar on planes, tour buses, cabs and cars across this country and a few others, as well. The hard shell of the case that protects my guitar has dents and cracks, and bubbles on the top that developed from over exposure to heat.

My guitar case shows the stress of touring for over ten years but what it protected, all that time, is still in working order. Yet, out of all the concerts I've done, songs I've sung and the countless personal appearances I've made, never once did I ever take my guitar out of its case and expect it to be in tune. Stresses and bumps and changes in the barometric pressure can all have a negative effect on the instrument. Unless I first take the time to tune it, the chords that I play won't sound the way the writer of the melody intended. We must submit to God's authority, the true "writer of the melody" for our lives.

How does one do that daily? I found the answer in the concept of "Know, Be, Do." That concept is for us to seek daily to "know" what God wants us to know, "be" what God wants us to be and then "do" what God wants us to do. It sounds simplistic in its concept but proves complex at times in its application. It comes down to believing it with all your heart and soul when you say "I want for me what God wants for me".

Section Five in my symphonic scenario is that we need to inculcate in our life the principal that Peter called Godliness. That means we are to obey Jesus without question even when it's inconvenient or seems unreasonable to do so.

In Luke 9:23 Jesus said "follow me." The disciples dropped their nets at the sea shore and, in reckless abandon, they followed. He did not preface that command with, 'follow me as long as it's convenient or if it only allows us to stay nestled safely in our comfort zone.' He simply said follow me.

The conductor of the symphony demands complete control of the dynamics, feel, and interpretation of the song He directs. God knows the song that is our life, better than anyone, because He composed it before time began. There was never a need for rewrites or changes because it was perfect from its inception. Our job in this daily walk with God is to listen as He sings the perfect lead, so that we might get in tune with it and add the harmonies for all to hear.

The sixth and seventh sections sit side-by-side in God's Orchestra Pit. They often play off of the same score of music in synchronized movement as is needed for that harmonious life which comes from God. Peter said we are to add "brotherly kindness" and in John 13:34-35 Jesus gave His disciples a new commandment. He said to "...love one another as I have loved you...." In that instant, Jesus set a new standard for how we are to love each other. Moses said, "Love your neighbor as yourself," but Jesus took it a giant leap forward. I believe that Jesus is making it clear here for all to see that He is the righteous standard, the bench mark by which brotherly love is to forever be measured.

We need to show other believers, in attitude and action, Christ's standard of love. Give others the benefit of the doubt. Take time to give to those in need as well as taking them at face value. Be slow to speak, slow to anger and swift to hear.

And, finally, the seventh section is to share Jesus' love. Show it through evangelism to the unbeliever and through mentoring our fellow brothers and sisters in Christ. "Iron sharpens iron" and, in John 15:8, Jesus says 'reproduce yourself.' Be a disciple maker by teaching others to analyze the number of empty chairs and un-contributing sections that may be present in the Spiritual Orchestra of their life. Be available to help them hear the "Maestro of Mercy" in order that they might follow His direction in their lives. When the symphony of our life, as written by God, is being played at its full "Fortissimo" or loudest point, that's where we'll find unspeakable joy and the peace that passes all understanding.

With the Orchestra of my life finally all in tune, I asked God, "What is it that You want me to do." He simply said, 'be faithful, be functional and be fruitful in the use of the gifts and talents I've given you. Write what I've engraved on your heart, - SING!' "What am I supposed to sing Lord," I asked. His answer to me was swift and over whelming. Sing the story of your life and describe how My Grace is sufficient.

As I began writing the song, "He Still Moves the Stone," other songs began flowing faster than I could write them down.

Chasing The Wind

Chapter 46

The True Message of Praise

Four months into my recovery from surgery, I had already written enough songs for two albums. I studied God's Word day and night and applied it to my life. I analyzed both the miracles I had seen, and the mistakes I had made, and carefully compared it to what God says about it in His Word, to find the message. With each application and understanding, a new song was born.

Christian music had changed so much while I wasn't looking. Praise and Worship and Vertical Music had become "catch phrases" of the day. Some music can only be described as 7-11 music; seven words repeated eleven times with an up tempo "boogie" beat. It had become so much more fashionable and politically correct to repeat a million times that "I am a friend of God, He calls me friend," and "My Redeemer lives," 47 times, than to sing one time about those nail pierced hands or The Old Rugged Cross. I missed the days of Dallas Holms and The Light House or Andrea Crouch's 'My Tribute' (To God Be The Glory) and 'The Blood Will Never Lose its Power.' These artists among many others of their day had songs that had a specific, intentional message. A life-changing message used to convict and draw people closer to God.

There's still a majority of Southern Gospel artist and a handful of Contemporary ones who still seek out that message in a song and measure it against the truth of God's Word before they ever agree to sing it.

We often get caught up in the frenzy of the hallelujah line and forget that at times we just need to be still and know that He is God. It's valid for us to open our mouths in order to let our feelings for God out as long as we don't forget to open our ears and hearts to let in His direction to us.

There is not a word of praise that we can say that the all Omniscient God does not already know. But there are countless things still left to be revealed to us by Him through music based on His Word. If others don't see Christ in us in our daily lives then the praises we offer up to Him on Sunday morning mean little. While it's true God is interested in our praises and promises, He is eternally interested in our position in Christ and the practice of walking with Him.

Christian music did not make this jump all on its own. It was ushered in with the rise of neo-evangelicalism in which the gospel has somewhat been watered down. The references to sin, the blood, the cross and an eternity in hell have been sadly minimized. I believe that if you're going to preach the truth, then for God's sake and our sake, preach the whole redemptive truth. Your best life now is not accomplished through the power of positive thinking and, no matter how purpose driven you are, without the forgiveness of sin by the blood of Christ on the cross, you will end up in the flames of hell, and I'm positive it will not feel like a sauna.

When Jesus walked, preached and taught among us on this earth, He didn't preach for applause, heal for money or promise us financial prosperity. In John 5:24 Jesus did, however, promise, "He who hears My word and believes in Him who sent Me has everlasting life and shall not come into judgment, but has passed from death into life." When the 'coin of the Realm' dripped from the cross, he purchased us out of the slave market of sin. So, because I'm secure, based upon what Christ did for me, I will remain content, looking forward to his return and those treasures that are laid up for me in heaven, according to my faithfulness. In my mind that's the only true Gospel of prosperity.

Chasing The Wind

Chapter 47

"That's What Fathers Do"

All song writers that I've ever known have their own way of creating and giving birth to a song. There are those who concentrate on the lyrics first, trying to get a flow in the words that fit some not-yet-conceived rhythm or feel. It becomes a poem, a group of rhyming words wrapped up in a rhythmical beat.

Some write the music first and then create the words to fit the number of beats per measure in the already created melody. The powerful parts in the written music dictate that the words should follow in a powerful way as well.

I have never been able to write music in either of theses forms or structural formats. When I sit down to write a song, words and melodies flow together simultaneously. I hear all the parts of the song, instruments, string arrangements, percussion as well as the harmonies. It becomes a complete picture in my mind from the first stroke of the pen.

There are times, however, when God provides mental flashes of unexpected creativity. That was never more in evidence than the day "That's What Fathers Do" was revealed. One day, I found myself contemplating how much I love my son and how the Bible says that our Father in heaven loves us even more than that. As I pondered His love for me and my love for Brock, together they quickly became the nucleus of a song that began to play over and over in my mind.

I thought about all the things that Fathers do for their children and how they're always there to wrap their arms around them and keep them safe and warm. I thought about how our Father in heaven loves us and how He keeps His promise to never forsake us.

As I heard the song take shape in my mind, I realized this could be a song that my nine year old son, Brock, could sing with me. The words would need to be pure and innocent so that even a child could understand the message. Then, out of the blue, God brought back to my mind something that I had not thought of in almost nine years.

I started searching through my list of recordings and tapes, trying to find what I immediately knew had been divine creation and planned for just this very moment in time. I went through box after box until I saw what I had been frantically searching for.

I grabbed the cassette and put it in the player hoping that time had not corroded the tape that God had providentially directed me to record for just this day. As the tape began to roll, I heard what I was hoping I would; the laughter of an innocent nine month old baby recorded back at SMART studios almost a decade before.

With one push of the play button I was instantly transported back in time to the smell of baby powder, chubby knuckles and dimpled cheeks. I heard the sweet, sparkling, melodious laughter from the very child for whom this new song would be written. Not only would his laughter set the tone and mood for the song but, this nine year old boy had now developed a voice of his own and could use his God-given talent to sing a portion of the song with his earthly father. It became a song about a father's love from heaven to earth, a message nine years in the making.

Why would God impress on my heart, all those years ago, to record and hold on to a tape that I had no reason to record in the first place. The only purpose for recording his "boisterous belly laugh" was so, someday, we could share it with his own wife and children. Back then, I had no way of knowing that my vision was so short sighted. God planned for me to share this baby's joy and innocence with the world.

For the next twelve months God restored my body as well as my faith. Half of that time I was confined to crutches and limited to non-weight bearing on my left leg. My body may have been constrained but my mind was not so, each day, I spent my time examining God's Word. Through the guidance of the Holy Spirit I grew stronger. I grew stronger physically, mentally and spiritually. I learned that there is sufficient Grace even in the face of insufficient faith.

When I was put to sleep for surgery this time, I didn't believe I would ever open my eyes again on this earth. When I asked my dad to take care of Nena and Brock just before they took me away, my request referred to more then just the rest of that day.

Dr. Lancaster, along with Dr. Medlock, did a great work on my broken hip, but what God fixed in me far exceeded their capabilities. I was broken in other ways, ways that could only be seen by God. As He painstakingly mended my broken dreams I began to feel spiritually, and inspirationally renewed.

That renewal was like a well, left empty and dry for so many years and then, suddenly, with a little divine digging and pressure, a new stream was struck. The soil at the bottom begins to turn dark as the water percolates up and spreads across the bed of the well until there is no other place to go but up and out.

Life-revitalizing water fractured the old well and, as it spilled out onto the dry and thirsty land, it seeped into every crack and crevasse of my spirit. It happened just that way and with each new song it just kept on flowing. I couldn't have stopped writing even if I wanted to.

Up, from what once was a dry hole, bubbled the songs of my life. Chasing the Wind, He Still Moves the Stone, The Storm Won't Last Forever, were just a few of the endless messages wrapped up in meter and rhythm. Songs meant to inspire others. Songs meant to remind me of where I'd been, who I was and where I was going. A musical "billboard," if you will, on the road of life for the lost and wounded. A sign that said, 'I've been where you are and I know the way back home. Stop Chasing the Wind and follow me; I know where rest can be found.

William Boyd Chisum

Chasing The Wind

Chapter 48

Moses and Me

For the first time in almost a year, I was able to physically return to my home church. Sunnyvale First Baptist had undergone a tremendous growth while we were away but its Pastor Charlie Wilson hadn't changed. Charlie gave God the glory for the church's impressive expansion and, as he stepped into the pulpit to preach, he was as inspiring and humble as he had always been.

So many Christians around this country have had a bad reputation of "shooting their wounded" instead of reaching out a helping hand or kneeling in sustaining prayer. For too many Christians, it seems castigation is much easier than restoration. Pastor Charlie wasn't that way. Charlie left the "stone throwing" to those who were blinded by the 2x4 in their own eyes.

When Charlie gave an altar call, which was at the conclusion of every meeting, he'd make it crystal clear. "There's no magic in the carpet that you step out on, the miracle happens right where you are and before that first step, it's done." No "hocus pocus," just Grace. With out it, we have no hope of anything.

The transformation taking place in my life from God's amazing grace was awesome to experience and witness. It could be described in two words; long overdue. When I looked in the mirror, I didn't appear to be different, but I was. Just like Moses, my wandering in the wilderness had changed me completely. Similar to Moses, I had been stripped of all the things that I thought were valuable in my life.

The three legged stool I sat on when I was performing country music so many years before had been self-built from fame, fortune and fans, and it crumbled into dust. The stool I built through my education in medicine rested on the legs of prestige, power and profit and it, too, got kicked out from under me by those precious sanctified sandals.

Like Moses in Exodus Chapter Two, this experience led me to "my own burning bush." I saw it when I opened my eyes expecting to see Jesus and saw "Recovery" instead. From that day on, I've never been the same. I had finally seen God's message for me and, just so I'd never forget it, I was busy writing it down.

I had been telling Nena's father, Jack, about all the things I had learned and about the songs that were pouring out of me, so he came to see and hear for himself. He sat at our breakfast table as I sang the songs God had laid on my heart. Tears rolled down his cheeks with every song and his excitement over the message was contagious. What do I do with all of this music Jack, I asked? How do I get God's message heard? "God will do that for you Himself. He will provide away" was his reply.

Jack was insistent that I record the songs but, he was equally insistent that I wouldn't need anything other than my guitar and voice to do that recording. "They don't need anything else," he kept saying. "But I hear so much other music in my head Jack," I said. Finally, over time, I was able to convince Jack that I had been inspired to write more than just the words and melody. There was power in each arrangement playing over and over in my head and I could not leave that up to the listener's imagination.

I began making preparations to once again step into a recording studio and sing. Unlike the countless times before, this time it was all about Him, His message, and His songs. I was only there to open my mouth and let it out. This time, however, there would be another voice added to the mix, the voice of my nine year old son, Brock.

Recording the "Chasing the Wind" album was a labor of love for everyone. From the engineers, Tom Cusic and Greg White to the musicians and background vocalists brought in to contribute their unbelievable gifts, everyone together gave it every ounce of talent they had to the Glory of God.

The day my son came into the studio to record his portion of the song, "That's What Fathers Do," was without a doubt the proudest day of my musical life. Nothing compared to the feeling I had watching him sing that night. All the awards, applause and fame paled in comparison. Nena, Jack and our engineer Tom Cusic all watched from inside the control room as I nervously helped Brock with his head phones. I carefully adjusted the microphone height so that it would catch every note he sang just right. If he was nervous it was only a little. He knew I was there in the room with him to coach him and lift him up to do the best job he could do. I believed in him and he felt my strength deep in his heart.

The wall that separated us from the control room was made out of solid glass approximately twelve feet high from ceiling to floor and easily forty feet in length. TM Century studio was a multi-million dollar studio and no expense was spared in its construction.

After going over the song to make sure Brock could hear himself and all the sound levels were where they needed to be, we sat back and watched a little nine year old boy perform like a seasoned professional. In only a couple of takes he was done. He gave me a look like, "Is that all there is to this recording stuff Dad?"

He was not intimidated at all. Brock provided a lesson for each of us that night, that "when there's absolutely no doubt, there's no holding back." If we had the faith of a little child, the faith of my nine year old son had that night, how much of the world could we change?

William Boyd Chisum

Chasing The Wind

Chapter 49

The Heavens Rejoice

God was not just revealing Himself to us through the creation and recording of the album. He was also making His saving presence known in the life of Brock.

One Sunday morning during the invitation at church, Brock grabbed Nena's hand as if he needed to ask or tell her something. As we both leaned down to hear he began to fumble and struggle with the words to express his thoughts. Finally, he gave up trying and said, "never mind." We knew that something was on his mind but we tried not to press him. He would come to us when he was ready. We didn't have to wait very long.

The very next Sunday, as we sat in our favorite spot down front where Charlie could keep an eye on us, Brock decided during the first stanza of the invitation to step out. He grabbed our hands and, together as a family, we went forward in order for him to make a public declaration that he had become a committed follower of Jesus Christ. There was no hesitation, no doubt but a sincere determination that he was following the Holy Spirit's calling and direction in his life.

He had come forward to make public his decision. He asked Jesus to come into his heart just fourteen days earlier and now he wanted to follow in believer's baptism.

Brock was scheduled for baptism in two weeks. The news went out, inviting everyone we knew to be a part of this special moment in his life. Brock understood that his baptism was simply a visual, public affirmation that Christ lives in him. There is no magic in the baptistery water either. The miracle is in the blood, nothing but the blood.

It's an inexpressible feeling to know that your child will one day spend eternity with you in heaven and that together you will worship at the feet of Christ. For a child who often worried about whether we were lost when driving in areas he wasn't familiar with, he would never again have to question where he was or where he was going. He was safe in the arms of God and he was passing through this life on his way to heaven. "Chucky Jesus" turned into precious Jesus and, through Him, Brock new his final destination.

The night of Brocks baptism, friends and family came from near and far. RoyDale came with his wife, Barbie, and their daughters, Deanna and Ashley. My mom and dad along with my cousin, Sandy, Nena's mom, Kaylla, were also in attendance.

Just before the service was about to begin I noticed Tom Cusic slip to the back of the auditorium. We had become very close during all the months of recording. He was an adopted member of the family now and Brock had made an indelible mark on him as well.

He had come, like so many others, to stand up for Brock and recognize his commitment to follow Christ. These people who were standing in his honor were the very people he could count on in the days and years to come.

Jack had previously asked Nena and me if he could have the privilege of baptizing his grandson. We thought it was a wonderful idea and Brother Charlie did as well. As I started to sing "That's What Fathers Do," Brock made his way into the baptismal waters.

At the end of the song, Brock took his Papa Jack's hand and, in obedience to His heavenly Father, was lowered beneath the water and then raised up to walk in newness of life.

It was a beautiful picture of Christ's death and resurrection in the life of our little boy. When he climbed to the top of the stairs his, momma was waiting. There wasn't a dry eye in the house as the whole congregation rose in recognition of all those who made decisions that night.

Chasing The Wind

Chapter 50

"Deja Vu All Over Again"

The album was finally completed and on its way to duplication. Jack had been busy setting up concerts for me in and around the Dallas area. I had made a commitment to God that I would go anywhere He opened the door for me to go. I was thrilled when one of those doors that opened took me back to my past.

First Baptist Church of Carrizo Springs, Texas was where I started singing a lifetime ago. I was going back to sing at my old home church for those who knew me when I was a child. More important than that was the opportunity to share the amazing things God had done in my life.

It was a special weekend planned for renewing old friendships. Ann Lansford, now Ann Blankenship, would be there with her family, to sing a few songs with me again. The concert was set for a Saturday night because I had a prior engagement on the night before. There was a Friday night high school football game and I had been asked to sing the National Anthem for my old school one last time.

Nena and Brock made the trip with me. This would be the first time Brock would sing in public. How appropriate that it would be in the same place, in front of some of the very same people, that I had tortured many years before. But, before I made it to Carrizo Springs, there was one stop I had to make.

I had located the whereabouts of Morgan Leeth, my high school band director. He and his wife, now retired, lived in San Antonio, Texas. Without question, I had to see them on my way down so I called and was given directions to their home.

As we drove up to their house, Mr. Leeth and his wife, Lynn, were waiting for us outside by the road. I couldn't get the car stopped and my seatbelt off before Mr. Leeth was at my door, opening it and wrapping his arms around me. Some bonds never fade no matter how long it has been.

He had not changed as much over the years as one would expect. He had a lot more snow on the roof than he did when I saw him last, but at least there was still some snow to be had. Because of our tight schedule, we couldn't spend as much time with them as I wanted but, over dinner, we took advantage of what time we had to catch up on old times. We left each other with an embrace and a commitment to stay in touch and said a prayer of thanks that we both had lived long enough to reunite once more.

As I stepped out onto the football field before kick-off that Friday night, a flood of memories washed over me. When I closed my eyes, I could see myself back in my purple and gold band uniform, standing at attention, waiting for the signal to sing. I once again felt the pride of representing my country and hometown welling up inside of me.

I was also reminded of my graduation when I stood, right where I was then, on the fifty yard line, and sang my heart out for the town and the people that I loved. The thought that I could be standing here, looking across the field at the hometown bleachers filled with some of the same people I saw a life time ago, was a vision I never expected to see again in my life.

The sound of whispers and murmurs brought me back to the present, and I took a quick glance over at Nena and Brock who were waiting in the stands for my name to be announced. I could hear people saying "that's Boyd Chisum out there on the football field. I can't believe he's here." Well, it had been a long time but life, all too often, has a way of coming full circle, and this was one of those times. As I began to sing I couldn't believe I was back here either. But God is good and He knew how much I needed this, He knew even more than I knew.

The concert at the church was set for Saturday night. Nena and I waited anxiously all day Saturday for Jack to make the six to seven hour drive from Dallas to Carrizo. He had stayed behind because the album had not yet come off the CD production line and he was supposed to bring the albums to the concert that night.

At around 3:00 p.m. Jack drove in with all the products for the concert. We were all set up for a "hot time" in South Texas that night. But the surprises just kept on coming.

When Nena and I took Jack to find his hotel, I ran into another childhood friend that dated back even further in my history than Carrizo Springs. Checking in at the same hotel, at the very same time, was Jan Penter. I used to watch her and her sister, Brenda, and her brothers, Ken and Ronnie, play baseball with my brother in our front yard back in Wake Village, Texas. We played together in those piney woods full of honeysuckle and grape vines. She had come to Carrizo Springs to surprise me and I truly was overwhelmed.

The concert that night was so exciting for me. Everywhere I looked I saw my history intermingled with my future; Nena and Brock sitting by Ann and Jan. The 'Bowling for Boyd' crew of Dave and

Kelly Dickey were busy helping Jack organize and manage all the various details of the concert. Preston Taylor came for awhile but he couldn't stay. He did, however, make sure that the posters that were put around town did not have his father's toupee tape attached to them. Ann sang with me a couple of songs, I sang about forty minutes worth of music and then Brock sang one song. With that one song, he stole their hearts and the show.

God moved in the lives of those who were there that night and, when we left, I knew lives were changed. Changed not by what I had done, but what God had done through me.

I had given back to the town who gave their love and acceptance to me. I had come home to say thank you for all those prayers for my life and to let them know, through it all, their prayers had been heard.

Now there was one other place left that I felt I needed to give something back to. One more circle that needed to be closed. I owed them more than I could ever repay, but God had a plan for that too, because He has always had a plan. I was just now starting to see that truth on a daily basis play out in my life.

William Boyd Chisum

Chasing The Wind

Chapter 51

Why Do People Suffer?

Why do people suffer? How is it that a loving God would allow bad things to happen to good people? We have all heard these sorts of questions before, pleading questions from those in pain who have encountered a tragedy in their lives or the lives of someone they know.

These were questions that I, too, have struggled with most of my life. We've all known someone who we felt was given a bad hand to play. Someone seemingly short-changed in life because the effort they put out didn't match the return they received. But we are simply looking at the situation through earthly vision, an earthly vision that, in the end, becomes deeply flawed by our lack of ability to see the "whole picture" being painted in the life of the one who's suffering.

There are many reasons why the believers suffer. Some undergo hardships because it's self induced. Others struggle through issues and trials to find a blessing waiting on the other side of their pain.

Some refuse to be broken by the will of God and, as a consequence of their on stubborn, arrogant will, end up suffering through His Divine discipline in their lives. But for some, their suffering is to demonstrate the almighty power of God. This form of suffering is often the hardest to understand or recognize. Over and over again we find this form of suffering wrapped around a life of pure innocence, the life of a child.

The blind man in John 9:6 and the paralytic in Mathew 9:2 had both been suffering since birth. They had been pitied, shunned and, since human nature hasn't changed in the last two thousand years, I'm sure they were laughed at and made fun of as well. I am quite confident that at different times in their lives they asked the question, "Why me Lord?" They had no way of knowing that all of their physical and emotional burdens were given to them to bear for that specific day in time -- that particular day when Christ made the power and strength of God obvious to all who witnessed His miracle through their weakness.

Self-induced suffering comes from "reaping what you sow." Gal. 6:7 says, "…for whatever a man sows, that he will also reap…." So many times we go around planting 'cockleburs,' expecting that, when it comes time for the harvest, we're going to be looking at strawberries. It just doesn't work that way. As Christians, some of our suffering is directly associated with the mistakes we make through the exercising of our own free will. If man's decisions had no consequences, then he would not be free. Bad decisions have bad effects. These bad effects cause us to suffer and often make us less effective in our efforts to become fully faithful, functional and fruitful followers of Christ.

In the Old Testament, King David was described as being the 'apple of God's eye.' But, after exercising his own free will concerning a certain Bathsheba and his subsequent confession, God forgave King David and restored him to fellowship. The Bible says that when God forgives He casts that sin as far as the East is from the West and remembers it no more. God does not keep a separate set of books to refer to past confessed sin in order to keep tally of our repeated mistakes. His sovereignty simply forgives and forgets.

Although the 'apple of God's eye' had been restored to fellowship, the natural consequences of his sin continued to have adverse affects. David's relationship with his family and children had suffered irrevocable damage and the nation of Israel had lost the glory that it could have achieved.

Even though David's own testimony had suffered, God still loved him, used him, and in the end God kept His promise of a royal dynasty to King David.

It's not a great stretch for us to understand how God could use a young boy who had just killed the 'Great Goliath' with a 'pocket full of rocks' and a slingshot full of faith, but God also used this man who, as a king, had become an adulterer and murderer as well. There are no sins or excuses in our past that could ever exclude us from the Grace of God.

Chasing The Wind

Chapter 52

In My Weakness He Is Strong

What does it mean to suffer for blessing? Why would God allow us to suffer (which to most everyone is a bad thing), in order for God to give us blessings which are good things? The answer to that question could be found in the life of the apostle Paul.

Paul was a great intellectual thinker. He had one of the brightest minds of his time. However, after he became a believer in Christ, Paul had to derive his power from God instead drawing from his vast knowledge or leaning upon his own understanding and comprehension.

It wasn't that Paul became an idiot the moment he believed in Christ. He still retained the superior intelligence and strong personality that he had back when he was persecuting Christians in his effort to stop the growth of the Christian Church.

To protect Paul against himself and to guard against Paul's propensity to rely on his own strengths instead of Gods strengths, Paul was given what he called a "thorn in the flesh".

In 2 Cor. 12:7-9, Paul wrote,
"And lest I should be exalted above measure by the abundance of the revelations, a thorn in the flesh was given to me, a messenger of Satan to buffet me, lest I be exalted above measure. Concerning this thing I pleaded with the Lord three times that it might depart from me. And He said to me, "My grace is sufficient for you, for My strength is made perfect in weakness."

God in His grace does not wait for us to fail. He is not a 'spiritual janitor' who comes in after the mess is made to sweep up our failures; God provides the means for keeping the believer from falling apart at the very start. He takes preventative action by often sending suffering for blessing. God's provision of suffering reminds the believer that he is dependent on God to get through the circumstances that human ability cannot resolve.

Paul's ministry probably would not have been effective without the disability that God gave him. God provides some believers with a disability to keep them humble as they accomplish great things in His name. Joni Erickson Tada, a quadriplegic from age sixteen, and Pastor David Ring, a great communicator of Gods grace who has suffered with debilitating cerebral palsy since birth, are just a couple of examples of this truth. They are living examples of Rom. 8:31b, "If God be for us, who can be against us?" Only the almighty God can turn suffering into blessing, and that blessing is delivered to us through fellowship with Jesus Christ.

Paul suffered intensely with his "thorn in the flesh" but even in the midst of the pain he sought relief and found it. Paul found sufficient grace and was lifted high by God's everlasting, infinite loving arms.

William Boyd Chisum

Chapter 53

Army of Love

It was early fall, Nena, Jack and I had just left a meeting at 2222 Welborn Street in Dallas, Texas. The luncheon we had just left at Scottish Rite Hospital had gone extremely well and we all had plenty of ideas on how to make the up-coming concert a success. We had just a little over eight weeks to put together a Christmas party for the kids that would be as special to them as the one I experienced that lonely Christmas many years ago.

The thing I wanted most was for the party to be about the kids and not about me coming to sing. All of that would be just a fringe benefit, a little footnote of history to what was the most important thing of all, those children.

I started planning and making phone calls as soon as we returned home. I was asking everyone who knew me and knew my heart, to come help make Christmas feel like Christmas for a child; especially one who may not be able to go home for Christmas this year.

Every phone call and contact I made promised they would try to help raise funds for the children's gifts or that they would go out and purchase them themselves. Churches and pastors and youth groups from all around Texas were mobilizing their congregations for this special effort.

Chris Kennard was a dynamic sold-out follower of Jesus Christ and we had become good friends while producing the Chasing the Wind album. He worked for the company that did all the preparation and duplication of that project. It was while working with him that we found out about his ministry. He had a Bible study and mentoring class with the young people at Lake Point, a ten thousand member church in Rockwall, Texas. As I told him of my plans for the party at Scottish Rite, he jumped at the chance for his kids to participate.

Nena and I had decided not to exchange gifts this year. We would spend what we would have spent on each other, for the kids. Many other people decided to do the same. My mother and father, who had benefited from the years of service and care that this organization had given to me, were more than willing to give back as well.

This was a great opportunity for my son, Brock. In fact, it would be a life lesson for all the youth who had said they would participate. They would all get to see up-close and in a very personal way that, for some kids, this world is not easy. For some, life is not just a "bird's nest on the ground." But I knew from experience what they didn't know; that those beautiful kids who others saw as being different, the kids who were struggling daily with physical challenges, were in fact truly different. They had living inside them a strength and courage unlike anything that the youth from Lake Point would have ever seen. If these wonderful kids from Rockwall would come, and look at these children of God, with their hearts instead of their eyes, I knew all the preconceived stereotypes would be torn down, and they would leave having received much more than they had given. But would they come? Would anyone come? Would I have enough presents to give all the children at least one gift? We all worked hard, planning and praying but, with the concert less than a week away, I still didn't know the answer to any of those questions.

Daily I asked that God would move in a mighty way and lay my burden for those kids on the hearts of all those people who were still trying to decide if they would participate. I wondered if those unselfish individuals, who came into an empty ward to pile presents in the bed of a lonesome little boy so many Christmases ago, worried as I was worrying now. If they did, I hoped my expressions of sheer joy and thankfulness in knowing I had been remembered made all their efforts worthwhile. With the party now just twenty-four hours away, I prayed that history would repeat itself, for all of us.

Some of Nena's co-workers and family members had donated several bags of toys. Together with the gifts we had gathered, I was beginning to feel a little more confident that I could give at least one present to each child. That confidence only grew when my mother and father showed up the night before the party with a trunk load of gifts of their own. I don't know how Mom got her hands on Dad's wallet, but I thank God that she did.

As we were sorting out all the gifts in age-appropriate piles, the door-bell rang. I went to the door and opened it to find a box weighing eighty-five pounds. The Fed-Ex guy who delivered it and carried it up the hill to my front door was obviously not as happy to see this box as I was. In my excitement, I forgot my own physical restrictions and picked the box up and carried it into the house. In the thrill of the moment, that box didn't weigh a thing.

Kelly and Dave Dickey from Seguin had come to the rescue once more. As we opened up the box, we were like little children. We marveled at God's perfect timing and precious provision. Then I received the phone call I had been waiting for. Chris Kennard and his whole youth group would load up in several church vans and meet us at the hospital the next morning. The wise men were coming, but this time they were only eleven to eighteen years of age and, hopefully, when they went back home, they would be much wiser.

I don't think Scottish Rite Hospital had any idea that an army of love this size would be coming up their driveway in just a few short hours. Like a child wrapped up in the excitement of Christmas, I couldn't sleep at all that night. There was a new star shinning down on Texas and it was illuminating the most caring place on earth that I had ever known.

William Boyd Chisum

Chasing The Wind

Chapter 54

Welcome Home

The sun was shinning bright that morning as we pulled into the Scottish Rite Hospital parking lot. Mom and Dad were in awe as they looked around at all that had changed. They had not seen this place since I was sixteen years old and the sight of its growth seemed to take their breath away. It was almost surreal to see them standing here again, on the same ground that once held their hope and heartache in its hands.

I could tell from the expressions on their faces as they looked around that they were reliving memories they probably wished could have stayed buried forever. Maybe opening old wounds for them would finally allow healing to take place. Maybe today they could irrevocably embrace the spirit of forgiveness for themselves and let go of any regret they might have over things they wished they had done differently. I know they did all they could do. I know they gave all they could give. The fact that we were all standing there together that morning, on those beautiful grounds, is proof enough that it was worth it. I knew, and have always known, they didn't have a choice. Now, maybe this day, they would, without doubt, know that too. It was time it was settled. It had to be done.

Shortly after entering the hospital, my self-proclaimed "go to girl," also known as the event coordinator, Betsy Yeckel, met us in the lobby. I had noticed on the way in, just to the left of the information desk, a sign that read 'We Welcome William Boyd Chisum back to Scottish Rite Hospital.' To the left of that sign was the bust of

Dr. Brandon Carrell. As I read the sign, I could not help but glance at him and somehow feel that the words I was reading were being repeated from somewhere up in heaven by the man who had done so much for so many. With a wink and a smile, I could hear him saying, "Welcome home Boyd, welcome home."

Betsy Yeckel had already prepared the stage and set up tables for us to unload all the gifts. The stage was located in front of a huge Christmas tree that must have been close to twenty feet high. In a circle around the stage area were countless poinsettias. Christmas was coming for the kids and it was only a couple of hours away.

The Audio Visual Department was busy getting the microphones and PA equipment ready for the concert. On two easels, one on either side of the stage, were enlarged posters of me when I was a patient there many years ago. Photos that Roger Bell, head of the audio visual department, had prepared so that the children would know that I was one of them and had been right where they are.

Seats had been arranged facing the stage and, with an hour still left before the concert was scheduled to begin, the crowd was already starting to fill the seats. The children would be the last ones to arrive. They would be brought down from their rooms in wheel-chairs and wagons and some would be brought in their beds. The best was saved for last. That's when the children would make their entrance, because this truly was all about them -- they were what brought me back.

I was fine tuning my guitar and in the process of getting prepared to start when I looked up to see Tom Cusic from TM Century coming in the door. He had video camera equipment and tripods under each arm. What a surprise it was to know this was as important to him as it was to me and Tom had come to get it all on tape.

While I was busy getting ready to sing, Mom, Nena, Dad and my cousin Sandy were all busy getting the toys out onto the three banquet tables that the "go to girl" had made available. The tables were loaded down with toys from end to end and stacked two feet high in some places. I could not wait to see the faces of all those children as they looked at the things that love had brought them.

Suddenly, I heard a large group of people come into the concert hall. It was Chris Kennard and the youth group from Lake Point. One by one they all filed by the table to add the gifts they had brought to the already overflowing "mass of fun that was just waiting for a child to happen".

The atrium where I had been set up to sing had a beautiful open-air feel to it. The strong smell of popcorn, that the volunteers had been popping all day, drifted across the room and its aroma only added to the party-like atmosphere. Some of the children were already coming in. Those who had been in the ongoing clinic would be the first to arrive, followed shortly by the ones from the ward.

There was a sense of excitement in the air as some of the people stopped to take a long look at the pictures on either side of the stage; pictures of a skinny little boy in traction, growing up in a building that no longer exists. The comparison from then to now was staggering and it left most people shaking their heads in disbelief. Was this the way it really was back then?

Finally the kids came down from their floors. In wheelchairs, beds, crutches and wagons they scattered out and, just as I had hoped would happen, the youth from Lake Point fanned out among them. The hospital children were almost all accompanied by a family member and, once again, I was struck by how much things had changed.

In sixteen years, my parents never had the chance to participate in a function of this kind. Thank God these parents today were able to spend as much time as they wanted with their child and never had to fear that dreaded voice on the intercom essentially saying, "You don't have to go home but, you can't stay here." I know she was just doing her job, whoever 'she' was that made that dreaded announcement every weekend, but we couldn't help but hate her with a purple passion.

William Boyd Chisum

Chasing The Wind

Chapter 55

A Place Called Grace

I sang for almost an hour. In between songs I talked to the kids and told them how loved they were in this wonderful place. I tried to encourage them that they could be anything and do anything in this world that they set their minds to. "The only limitation you have," I said, "is your own imagination."

I told them, "You are special and never let anyone tell you different. When times get tough in your life, and they will from time to time, just remember, it's not the number of times you fall down but how many times you get up that count," I said.

I could not do a concert in this place without asking a certain someone to sing with me. I know that all day she had been thinking of the first time she signed me over to this place and then had to walk away. My parents had as much of a history here as I had. I am sure I will never know the full extent of that history. Mom and I sang a duet together to show the parents in attendance that there is a light at the end of the tunnel and that, through Gods grace, they too will one day stand together and say, "We did it. We made it through."

The last song that I sang for them that day referred to a 'new star shinning.' For me, that star was this new place where all the staff is dedicated to the health and happiness of children. This place that treats over 16,000 precious kids each year at no charge to the patient's families is truly, without a doubt, a gift from God. It was our shelter in the storm when there was no place else to turn and it is still providing healing, hope and love for so many children today.

With the last of my last vocal note fading away in the distance, I finally said the magic words that all the children there had been waiting to hear, "Let's hand out the presents." There was a mad rush on the tables. It was like an 80% off sale at Wal-Mart. All the volunteers who had come to give presents away had their hands full, making sure that every child received at least three gifts each. God had blessed us in the toy drive beyond measure and now came the payoff. The smiles and the 'oohs and aahs!'

There was a little boy who was all wrapped up in a blanket, lying in a little red wagon. He had undergone surgery on his arm just the day before and had only now returned from clinic where he had been placed into a long arm cast.

I had seen my dad talking to this little boy off and on all evening. I could tell my dad saw a strong resemblance between him and his own little boy many years ago. I made my way over to where he lay in his little wagon. He had not made it to the table for a present yet, so I wanted to see if I could find something he would like.

He had been in pain all through the concert, but his mother said that he refused to leave. She told me he loved music and that he had a guitar at home as well. His sweet spirit and beautiful blue eyes touched my heart but it absolutely stole my father's. I don't think he will ever forget little Trent and how he suffered through to receive the blessing that God had in store for him that day.

As Nena was working behind the gift table, she noticed a sixteen year old boy picking up several gifts and putting them back. He was looking for just the right thing and was determined not to settle for anything less. After carefully selecting three or four presents, he looked up at Nena and asked, "Can you take me back to my room?" Nena said, "Absolutely. If you can show me the way, I'll take you there." Up they went in the elevator to his floor, all the while, sharing small talk. She rolled him into his room and, as she was leaving, she said "I hope you had a good time at the party and I hope you found what you wanted on the gift table." "Oh these presents aren't for me," he said. "They're for my family. I picked these for my dad and my two brothers. I have been in here for so long that I haven't been able to buy presents for them this year. I couldn't have Christmas without being able to give them something."

This young boy had not gotten himself anything from the table. His only thought was of his family. There were plenty of presents there for him to have picked something for just himself. Nena tried to explain that to him and offered to go back down and bring him something, but he wouldn't hear of it. He was completely content with the choices he had made.

We had put this concert together so that we could give something back and a young sixteen year old boy had used it to do the very same thing. I hope and pray that someday his family will know how he demonstrated to us his unselfish love for them.

After the crowds had faded and everyone was in the process of cleaning up, I was approached by Roger Bell. "Would you or could you take a moment and come back to our department and let us do an interview with you on camera? We also have folders of pictures that were taken back in the old hospital and maybe you can identify some of the people in them for us." I was thrilled to have the chance to tell the story of what this place had done for me.

After saying goodbye to Chris Kennard and the kids from Lake Point and thanking them for making this a day to remember, my mom, Jack and I headed back to Roger's department for the interview.

I spoke about my love for this place and how much Dr. Carrell meant to me. I told stories as if they happened yesterday because this place was my childhood and it's easy to recall the times in your childhood when you've felt loved and happy.

The interview went on for almost forty five minutes. I recalled the good times and the bad times as well. I wanted it to be on tape, just how things were for all of us back then. It needed to be written down somewhere for future generations to see and learn from us. I wanted everyone to know we had no bad times, because we had nothing to compare it to. This life was all we knew but, in contrast to today, this 'new star' shining was brighter than I ever could have dreamed.

With the interview over, we went back to pick up our things and to say goodbye. It had been an unbelievable day and I hoped that God had used me in some way to encourage those children to seek Him and His strength. We started to leave but there was one more thing I needed to do before we left.

Just a short walk from the entrance of the hospital, nestled between several white oak trees, I found what I was looking for. Standing where she had stood for as long as I could ever remember, was my beautiful white statue.

My parents had to have a few pictures of me in front of her. After all these years, nothing had changed regarding that tradition. After the photos, they moved away and I was thankful to have a few moments alone with my thoughts.

William Boyd Chisum

As I stood where I had stood countless times before, I thought of all the things in my life that had come and gone. I reflected on all the things I'd lost along that winding road. A road of my own making that, over time, lead me straight back to this place.

I had chased the wind and gained nothing. I had pursued fame and fortune and had left, in its jet stream, broken lives, broken hearts, and broken dreams.

I chased the wind to find medical knowledge and, in the end, found nothing but a vision that I could not resuscitate. But it was when I planted my feet in the 'solid rock' that I finally broke free from the wind.

When you reach the point where you're ready to stop "Chasing the Wind," you'll look around to find that you've arrived at a place called 'Grace,' and I'm living proof, that it's sufficient.

Log On To Get Your FREE Bonus CD!

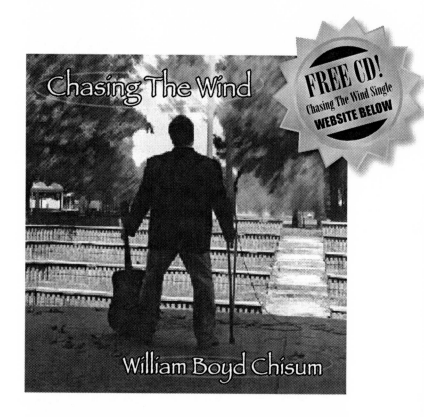

available at:

www.Morgan-James.com/chasing

A portion of the proceeds derived from the sale of each book will go to enhance the lives of the children at Texas Scottish Rite Hospital for Children in Dallas Texas. Their strength inspires us all.

In His Sufficient Grace,
William Boyd Chisum

Instructions on how to receive your FREE bonus single:

To receive your FREE bonus single of the song "Chasing the Wind", go to www.morgan-james.com/chasing. Click on the Chasing the Wind Bonus link and then fill out the required information. The password for your free download of the single "Chasing the Wind" is: Just One Touch.

To learn more about the ministries of William Boyd Chisum and how you can schedule him for a concert at your church or as a motivational speaker for your corporate or civic event, be sure to visit his website at www.williamboydchisum.com or contact Jack Moulton at Moulton Management by phone at 1-888-MOULTON or by e-mail at jaxcorp@comcast.net

My Statue

Courage comes in all sizes

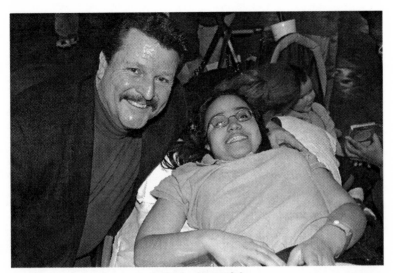

Isn't she beautiful

Christmas smiles

Keith

Dorothy Chisum and Boyd with a very young TSRH patient

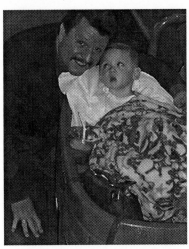

William Boyd Chisum and Trent

Printed in the United States
216473BV00001B/3/A